KMS Twelve Chapters about a Design Office.
By Conway Lloyd Morgan

avedition**rockets**

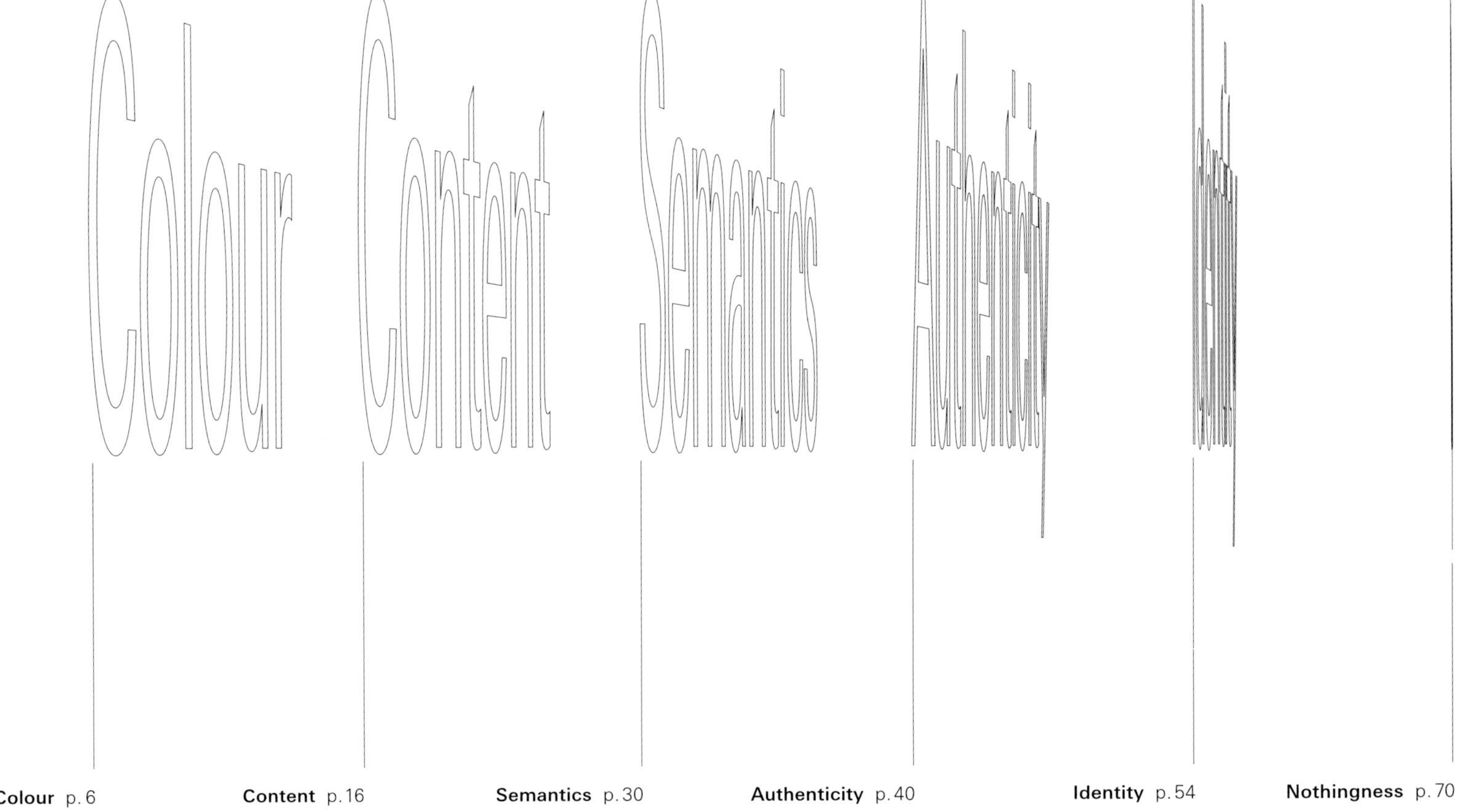

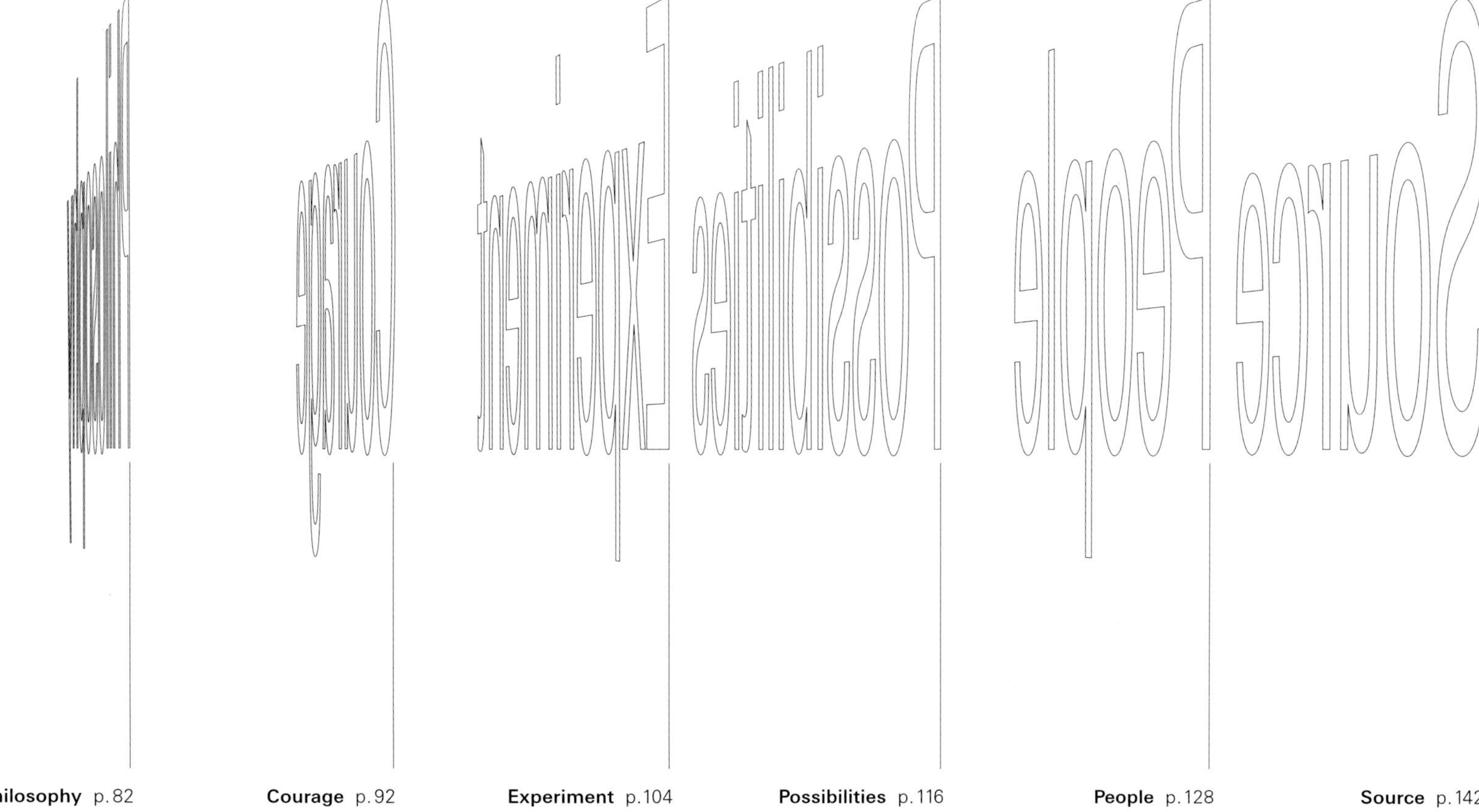

"A noir, E blanc, I rouge, U vert, O bleu, voyelles,
Je dirai quelque jour vos naissances latentes"
Arthur Rimbaud, Voyelles

feisty

Colour So you want to know what colour that is? Simple, isn't it? Hue, value and chroma are all you need. Munsell will even give you a number for it. If that isn't enough, ask your friendly local physicist to measure the wavelength and you'll know exactly what colour it is. The ancient Greek poet Homer did not have colour charts or a spectroscope, but that did not stop him trying to use colours descriptively, often as adjectives paired to nouns or names. The goddess of Dawn has rosy fingers, and a glimpse at the eastern sky shows why. But he also called the colour of the sea 'oinopos.' This is traditionally translated into English as 'wine-dark', whatever that may mean. (In the Iliad Homer also uses the adjective to describe the colour of oxen, if that helps. In pre-classical Greece wine was — probably — red and oxen were dark brown.)

Homer's strange phrase and Munsell's exact numbers are both incomplete. In scientific terms colour is an objective phenomenon: the spectrum is the range of wavelengths of light visible to the eye. But, whatever Munsell says, the spectrum has no discrete points to it: colours and tints shade into each other like a flowing river. So any communicated understanding of colour is effectively subjective, not only because of the limitations of language and constraints of culture but also because of the individual quality of each human eye. Colour is thus not so much a phenomenon as a language. The human eye can distinguish twelve thousand separate colours, but most languages only have specific names for ten or twelve, relying thereafter on

qualifiers 'deep blue', 'pea green', 'reddish brown'. Or on words whose sense we can no longer attain …
Each individual 'named' colour in turn carries a welter of associations and connotations, both individual and social, that affects our understanding. The colour red, for example, is commonly supposed to stimulate hunger, green is allegedly calming. Move across cultures, and in China red stands for luck, in America for danger, in Russia, once, for revolution.
Colour is an essential element in any design (even for black type on white paper.) But colour does not have a fixed meaning or a finite understanding. So design embarks from the start on a sea of ambiguity—a wine-dark one.

Inhalt
„Ein bedeutender Vorteil des Zusammenschlusses ist die bessere Positionierung von Sa
innerhalb der Gruppe."
"An important benefit originating from
enhanced positioning of Sat.1 and ProS
Kempen & Co
Joost van E
12

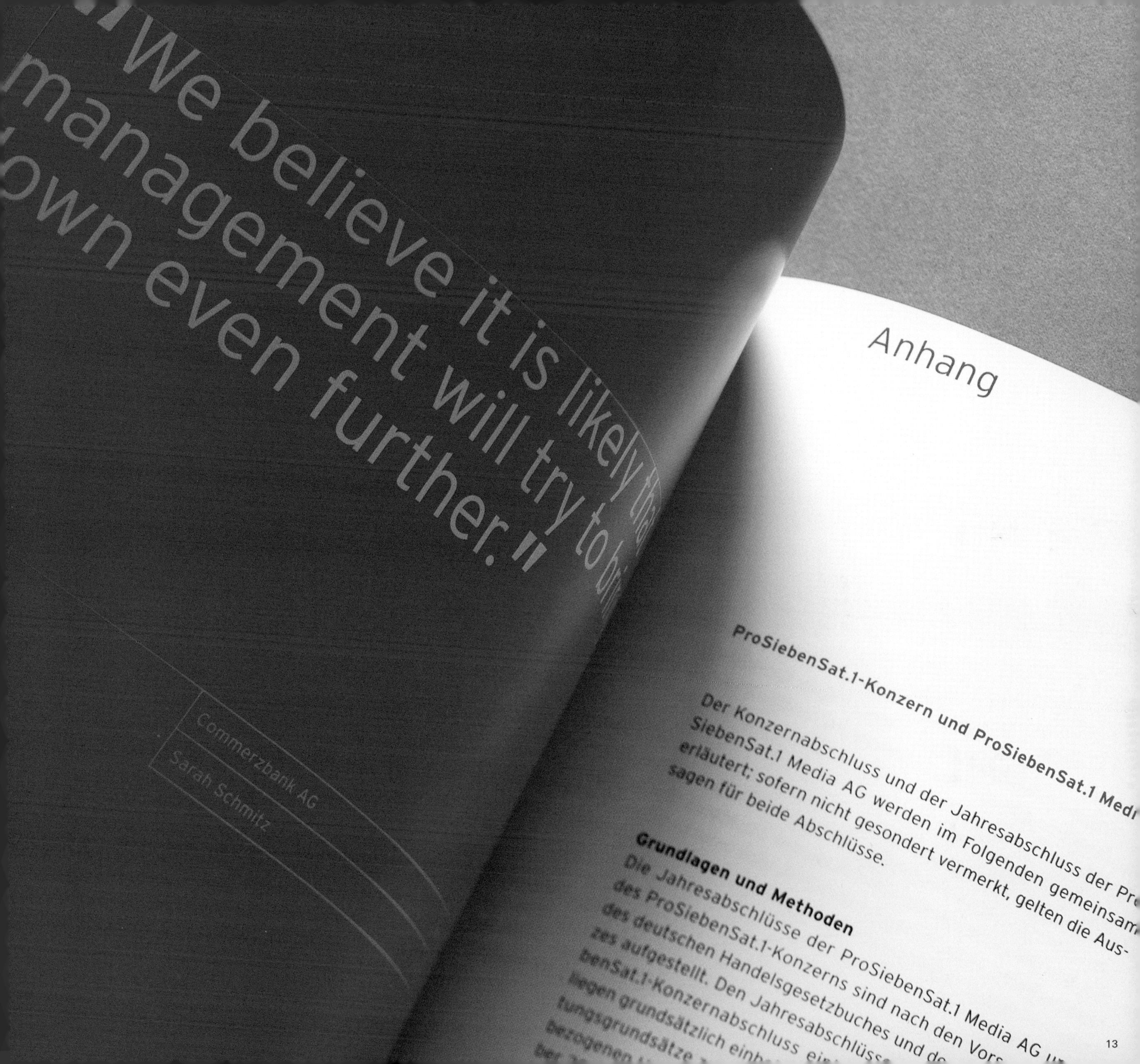

Anhang

ProSiebenSat.1-Konzern und ProSiebenSat.1 Media AG

Der Konzernabschluss und der Jahresabschluss der ProSiebenSat.1 Media AG werden im Folgenden gemeinsam erläutert; sofern nicht gesondert vermerkt, gelten die Aussagen für beide Abschlüsse.

Grundlagen und Methoden

Die Jahresabschlüsse der ProSiebenSat.1-Konzerns sind nach den Vorschriften des deutschen Handelsgesetzbuches und des ProSiebenSat.1-Konzernabschluss und de... liegen grundsätzlich ei... fungsgrundsätze z... bezogen...

Client ProSiebenSat.1, Munich
Project Annual report 2001

Brief In the profound crisis facing the media industry as a whole the client had also had a difficult year. The report should emphasise their determination to manage the crisis successfully. In addition, the report should show that ProSiebenSat.1 had emerged as one of the most important television service providers in the German market.

Concept The starting point for the design was the use of comments from independent analysts to clarify and validate the current market situation and the company's response. This determination, and the information contained in the report, needed to be presented in an attractive and relevant manner, and for this a magazine concept was the solution. This approach is very evident in the illustrated information sections, like feature articles relating to different aspects of the client's business: programme development, film-making, co-productions, trade fair presentations, viewer statistics and so on. Commentary from the board of directors is treated like editorial, while contemporary quotes and comments from independent analysts are used as headlines in each section opening. The abstract cover design, with its strapline 'For New Challenges', expresses the determination of the client, and the report opens with four double page spreads, each featuring a program from one of the channels the client operates, and again linked to an independent comment. The opening pages also use a graphic lattice developed from the client's corporate mark.

Comment The use of external expert voices from the financial world is unusual, but seems to have attracted the attention of the readers of the report.

"The closer the expression is to the thought, the more indistinguishable
the word from the content, the more beautiful is the work."
Gustave Flaubert, letter to Louise Collet

Content Nos dawch: until I sat down to write this, I didn't know how those words were spelt. But their sound and their meaning (they are the Welsh for 'good night') have been known to me since my childhood, and I used to say them to my children, when they were younger. Now, I didn't feel I was breaking some kind of link of memory in putting the words on paper, or putting memory in danger, but it did make me reflect on why we insist so much on verifying our knowledge through setting things out or writing them down.

It must be about authentication, confirmation and definition, all at the same time. But writing the words down does change the ordering of memory: what had been a sound now becomes a text, as well. I may have verified the spelling of the words (and so confirmed that my memory was correct.) But as the phrase above moves from my memory, onto my screen, then onto your paper, the context in which that content exists subtly and inevitably changes. And such changes of context impinge on content, on what we know about what we know.

Modulating the context not only can make the content more transparent, it also empowers the user of the context to select their own view of the content: you now know how to say good night to someone in Welsh! The person modulating the context can set their own levels of interference to the user's freedom, up to totality (suppose I had just written 'nos dawch' without any translation or explanation: in one sense not even I would have known what I meant, let alone you or anyone else.) So while totality breaks communication, anything less than totality creates discourse. We share what I know.

In the same way, the content of a design is modulated by its inclusion in the design. Even a photograph that becomes a poster changes. Not simply is its visual appearance subtly modified by a different reproduction process, but its status changes, from image to icon. The duty of the designer towards content is towards transparency, towards a maximum of discourse. But not a totality of discourse either. Totalities are about eclipse, after all.

Marbach Cursive

Concept for a Museum of 20th Century Literature
Translated from the German
by Philip Mann

1.   Basic Considerations

Literature does not lend itself easily to exhibitions. Unlike pictures, for instance, the objects commonly associated with literature were not usually designed to be put on show. While vision is the physical precondition for reading, it is a cognitive process and is ultimately independent of its material coding. Moreover, most of the classic vehicles of literature are relatively unspectacular (unlike other objects, e. g. garments, musical instruments, weapons or other artefacts which often develop great aesthetic appeal independently of their actual purpose). Apart from really magnificent specimens or masterpieces of calligraphy, the uninitiated will find little to marvel at in a book or a manuscript.

It would nevertheless be wrong to try to 'help' literature by using communication methods which, however well-intentioned, are alien to its nature; because after all, as a "secondary, modelling semiotic system" (Lotman), literature itself presents physical and intellectual reality through the medium of language. The result would always be counterproductive, because such attractions would always overlay the less sensual art of language, thus implicitly disparaging it.

On the other hand, there is unanimity concerning the great importance which attaches to graphic clarity and sensuous experience in any kind of exhibition. In an age with such a rich diversity of media and cultural offerings it is more than ever essential to find a modern form of presentation which will interest a broad target group. Without wanting to toady uncritically to the entertainment industry, the importance of the topic 'literature' should be underscored by an appropriate treatment which is attractive for the visitor. The concept described here is intended as a proposal for a form of presentation which develops artistic devices from within, i.e. from the essence of literature, and thus itself remains, figuratively speaking, literary.

1.1   The Typography Principle

The book serves as an abstract basic idea and frame of reference for design and communication. In a nutshell, the central idea of the concept may be formulated thus: the museum is itself a book.

1.1.1 The Book as Point of Departure and Chief Metaphor

Even though literature occurs in an extraordinary variety of guises, not even the written form being a necessary precondition, in our society the book may be regarded as the object with the most obvious literary symbolism. As a tangible and visible object the book has a very special attraction. This aspect is particularly in evidence in a museum whose inventory includes many bibliophile and historically valuable editions.

Our basic communication concept aims to eliminate the separation of visitor and object, which is typical of exhibitions, in such a way that a visit to the museum could be more readily compared with actively reading a book (i.e. the original literary experience) than with passively looking at objects (which in this case happen to be associated with literature).

This implies not a mimetic, but an intellectual transfer, which is crystallized in concrete details, by adapting book-specific principles—type area, the turning of pages—to different aspects of the exhibition.

1.1.2 Type Area as Organizational Scheme

With regard to design, the concept has to:
be in keeping with the nature of the exhibits
create clarity and uniformity
combine aesthetic attractiveness with artistic restraint
be appropriately anchored in the context of 'literature'.

These characteristics can be interpreted as classic functions of type area and typography. Just as the various elements of a book (text, headings, page numbers, table of contents, illustrations etc.) appear in a regularly arranged and hierarchical manner, so also the contents of the museum are organized: General explanatory texts, the labelling of exhibits, the navigation system, the display cabinets and the exhibits themselves follow a pattern whose abstract model is the book.

1.1.3 "Marbach" Typeface

One means of expressing the integral exhibition concept would be to develop a special Museum of 20th Century Literature typeface, the "Marbach". It would point to the traditional relationship of the Schiller National Museum and German Literature Archive to typography and bibliographic art, as is apparent in the "Marbacher Magazinen", and at the same time to the prominent role played by typography in 20th Century literature.
The "Marbach" would create a strong formal link between exhibitions and catalogues, and would have a public impact as an identifying feature, i.e. a kind of corporate design.

1.2   Topography Principle

As the "most critical of the Arts" (Invitation to Tender, p. 50) literature needs a form of exhibition which conforms to this spirit. No interpretation should be imposed on visitors. Rather, they should be able to control their reception of the exhibition as they see fit.
On the other hand, this must not result in exhibits simply being put on show without any organizational principle. In times of dwindling familiarity with the literary tradition and a decline in the reading habit, it is more than ever necessary to offer aids to orientation and, via an open and clearly structured communication concept, to provide approaches to literature for those visitors who do not feel they are experts.
Independently of the guided tours offered, the appeal of the visit should be increased for those visitors who are not connoisseurs or aficionados of literature—school classes, excursion groups, educated members of the general public. This can be accomplished by a flexible concept which allows independent investigation but none the less offers sufficient support.

1.2.1 Visit to the Museum as a Sightseeing Tour

A sightseeing tour of a town seems a useful analogy for an exhibition concept of this type. In both cases, visitors with different levels of knowledge of the subject and different interests have to be catered for. Accordingly, a good 'tour guide' should offer various exploration options. These would certainly include the compact tour of the principal sights, but also a selection of routes each focussing on a particular aspect: architecture, museums, shops, restaurants etc. As a matter of course, these routes will repeatedly intersect and to some extent be identical. And every visitor, depending on his or her temperament, available time and interests, will more or less keep to a suggested itinerary or make spontaneous detours.

1.2.2 The Path System

Literature is not a linear process, but a complex weave of interrelationships, intertextual references and extraliterary influences. Hence it seems appropriate for the Museum of 20th Century Literature to offer different thematic paths through the century, representing the almost infinite variety of possible approaches and links. Literary history may be told on the basis of outstanding authors and works or as a sequence of more or less clearly definable epochs. It may be read as a record of the history of ideas, as a seismographic echo of socio-political developments, or as a testimony of intellectual (and frequently also actual) resistance to suppression and violence. However, the century can also be reviewed in a way that is based on the inner workings of literature itself: tracing the development of a literary genre, a changing motif, an underlying theme or a debate on the principles of poetics.
Our exhibition concept is in keeping with this variety of possible paths. Rather than on a single, partially curtailable tour, it is based on a representative selection of relevant lines of development which are then linked to form a polyphonic system of complementary sub-exhibitions. Each path produces a unique, self-contained 'story'; every such story also reflects the whole (cf. 2.3). The individual stages on a path form thematic foci where lines can intersect, fork off or be reunited.

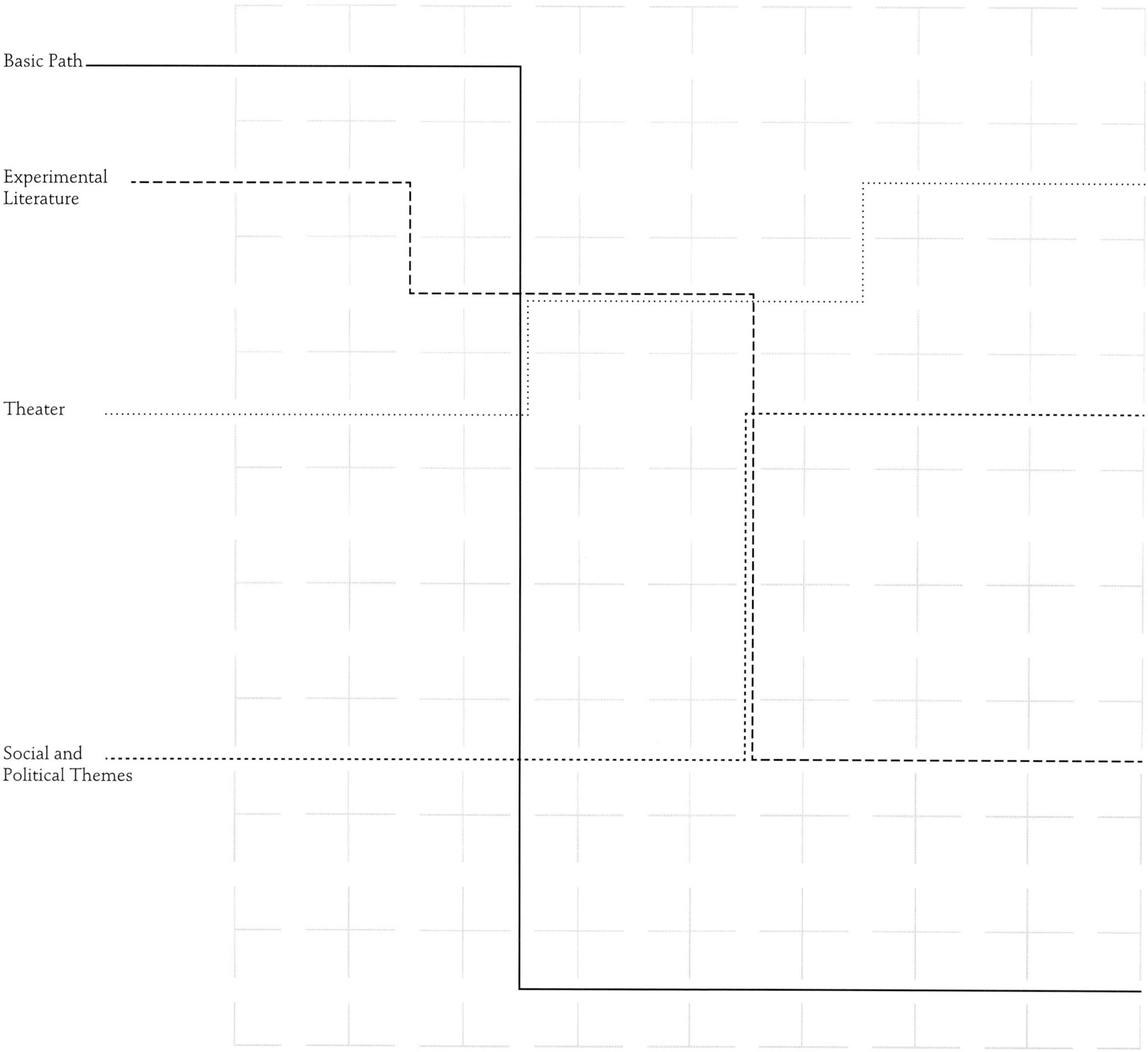

Basic Path

Experimental
Literature

Theater

Social and
Political Themes

1.2.3 The Emancipatory Museum

The concept aims to be a logical further development in the 'Marbach' tradition of a "'discursive' type of exhibition" which does not seek to "stage", but exploits the semantics of the exhibits in such a way that "a story always develops, through contrasts and antitheses, through mutual 'commentary' or through direct correspondence" (Invitation to Tender, pp. 53f.). The principle of intelligent relationships, the connection between which is revealed by an active reception attitude, has replaced the 'lecturing' presentation of canonized contents which presupposes a passive (and hence implicitly immature) visitor.

The path system makes this attitude explicit by institutionalizing options. On the one hand, the criticism that exhibitions demand "too much expertise and receptive effort" can be countered by a clear 'lay-friendly' strategy for conveying information (cf. 2.2.3 and 2.6). At the same time, the paths symbolize the primacy of the individual decision and approach. Semantic connections find expression in spatial contiguity, representing the precondition that, ideally, every visitor will experience his or her very own version of the history of 20th Century literature.

2 Exhibition

2.1 Building

[…]

2.2 Modules

The basic elements of the interior design derive from the image of a stylized book (open and stood upright). These corners inform the entire museum; four of them define a room.

The modular rooms accommodate the stages on the exhibition paths. By virtue of their design and configuration they allow a variety of routes and thus also different combinations and connections. At the same time, each room, despite its permeable structure, will also be perceived as an independent unit. Thus the different themes can each be given their own communicative emphases, as appropriate for the contents (cf. 2.4).

The resulting variations on a formally fixed and recognizable basic pattern will lend the exhibition a liveliness without confusing or distracting. The sequence of rooms with changing 'characters' will arouse the visitor's natural curiosity; the openings, allowing glimpses but not revealing everything, will reinforce this effect.

2.2.1 Walls

Each module has a square ground plan, with sides five metres long. It is enclosed by wall units four metres high and two metres wide, placed at right-angles to one another. An opening one metre wide will be left in the middle of each side. This opening can be replaced with a corresponding wall unit to create continuous five metre long wall surfaces if required.

It will be possible to vary the positions of the wall elements so that changes in the museum can be made at any time. The units can also be used for external exhibitions.

2.2.2 Positioning of Display Cabinets

A 40 centimetre wide band will run across each wall unit at eye level. It will be designed as a sill-like recess into which the display cabinets (or additional units, see 2.2.4) can be hung. An engaging mechanism will enable the cabinets to be moved easily, by means of a trolley specially built for the standard height. The trolley can also be used to transport exhibits and in the archives.

All display cabinets will be 40 cm high and deep, and one or two metres wide. Placing them on the walls of the room module will create an impression of spaciousness.

The central space can be left vacant or used to present particularly outstanding and valuable exhibits. These will be displayed in cabinets, likewise placed at eye level by means of pedestals or suspension devices, so that they also conform to the 'type area' of the wall cabinets.

2.2.3 Text Levels

In each room, information will be provided on four clearly graded levels: the 'Room Text' will state the theme and give a brief general introduction to it. It will be the only standard element to be placed outside the display cabinet bands.

Each cabinet will have a 'Cabinet Text' explaining the context of the exhibits displayed in it and, in turn, putting this into the wider context of the room theme.

For each exhibit, a short text will be provided which, apart from a precise identification or bibliographic details, will include the essential information regarding the context presented in the cabinet.

All secondary explanations and information will be provided not only by the catalogue, as customary in the past, but also in digital form, accessible in the immediate context of the exhibition (see 2.6).

2.2.4 Arrangement of Exhibits in the Cabinets

The principle of clarity and reduction also applies to the arrangement of exhibits and text in the display cabinets, because these will be a particularly sensitive area of perception in the exhibition. Insufficient spacing, positioning of the exhibits in different ways, non-uniform placement of explanations, and collective labelling quickly give the impression of crowding and confusion. Visitors who are less familiar with names, titles and relevant facts will feel overtaxed by such constellations.

We suggest that the cabinets themselves, and the exhibits displayed in them, be arranged according to a uniform pattern. With the exception of busts etc., for which separate solutions must be found, exhibits will be presented uniformly on a sloping 'floating' surface, with a brief caption on the floor of the cabinet directly in front of each exhibit. A general explanation of the cabinet theme will be printed on the rear panel of each cabinet.

2.3   Paths

Visitors will be able to choose from several thematic paths; or alternatively, to visit the individual modular rooms in the museum in whichever order and however thoroughly they wish, according to their own knowledge and interests or to decisions prompted by the exhibition.

2.3.1 Basic Path

A Basic Path will be provided for a visit lasting approx. 45 minutes. The path will cross the rooms whose themes are the 'milestones' in literary history—be they genres such as Expressionism or Kahlschlag, politically occasioned phenomena such as exile, Innere Emigration or GDR literature; great names such as Kafka, Mann, Brecht, Celan; or central works such as Der Untertan (The Patrioteer), Berlin Alexanderplatz or Die Blechtrommel (The Tin Drum).

2.3.2 Thematic Paths

As an alternative to the Basic Path, and repeatedly crossing and overlapping it, Thematic Paths also lead through the century. Based on the concept of a dense web of links and relationships, they will trace various lines by way of example, not as absolute patterns of interpretation. For instance, one path could be devoted to the socio-political conditions and subjects of literature; another could deal with innovation and experimentation; and a third defined by interrelationships with scientific and technological debate. All three would cross, for instance, the 'Naturalism Room', the two last-mentioned the 'Berlin Alexanderplatz Room', and the two first-mentioned the '47 Group Room'; while a room for documentary-political literature (Enzensberger, Hochhuth, Kipphardt, Böll) would be a stage on both the first- and last-mentioned paths.

There are, naturally, countless other possibilities. A 'Poetry—Drama—Narrative' triad would be just as plausible as a subdivision into topics bearing on identity, such as gender differences, origins or social class. For this reason also, it would be conceivable and appealing to change the permanent exhibition from time to time by rearranging the Paths.

2.3.3 Temporary and Showcase Exhibitions

Ideally, a temporary exhibition would be fully integrated in the Path system, i.e. the modular rooms reserved for it would create a Path dealing monographically with the theme, but at the same time relating it in multiple ways to the rest of the museum.

Thanks to the modular structure, however, a complete separation would if necessary also be possible, by selecting the rooms for the temporary exhibition together, as a separate unit.

This also applies mutatis mutandis to the Showcase Exhibition. Alternatively, it could be accommodated in the modular rooms on the ground floor, thus giving it a gateway function.

2.4   Presentations

Within a modular exhibition system, themes and exhibits can be given subtle and varied emphasis. Merely by specific selection, arrangement and commentary, each room takes on an individual character, which is underscored by the staging chosen for it. With relatively low technical input in some cases—projection of texts

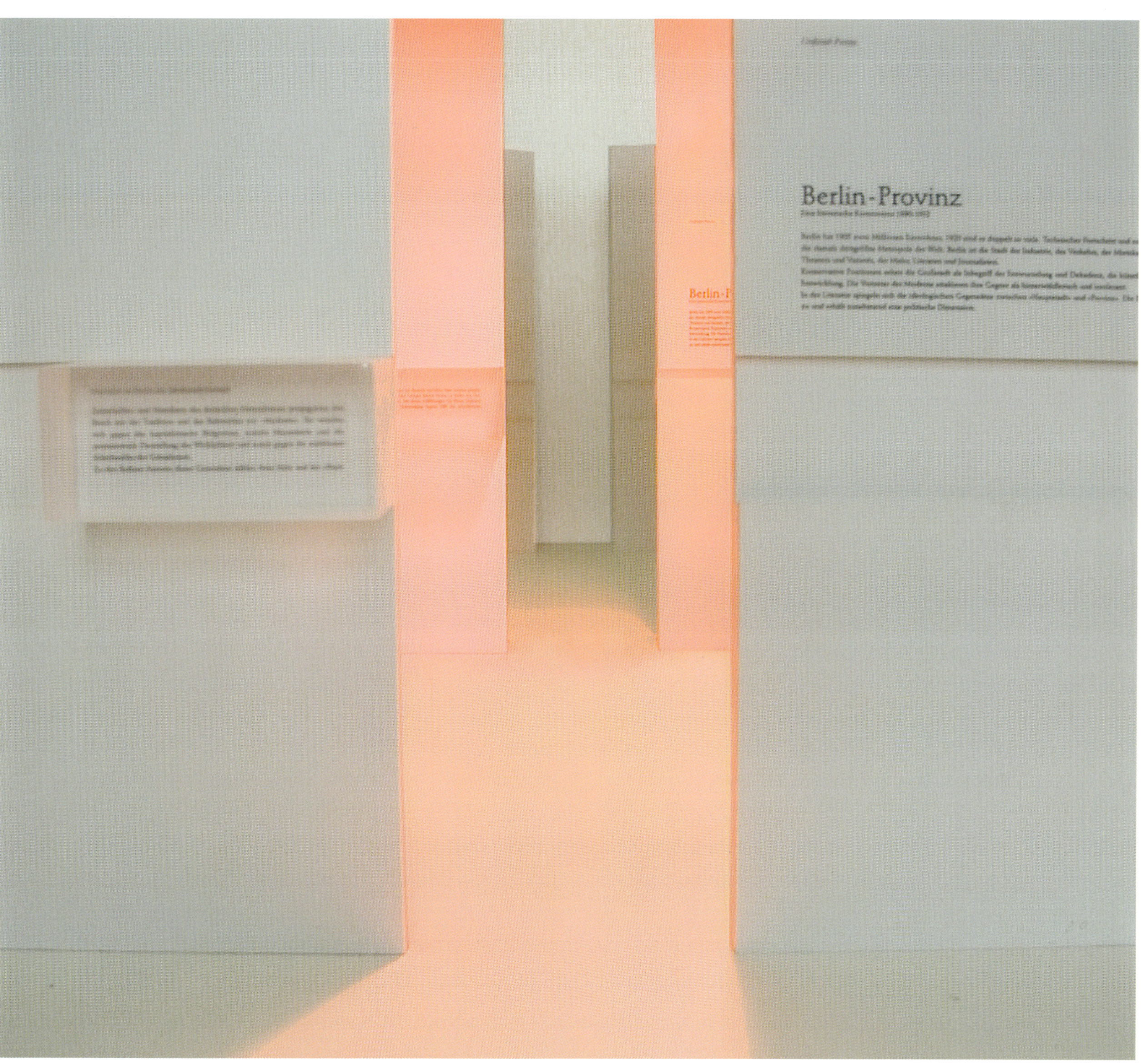

onto the walls, organization of the centre (with a suspended cabinet, pedestal or recess), coloured light—particular aspects of the subject can be reflected symbolically and/or sensually. A controversy can be illustrated with selected quotations at corners; a colour mood can suggest a particular attitude towards life (e.g. blue for Expressionism), and placement of an exhibit in the centre will automatically indicate its importance.

Due to their size, the rooms can be almost completely sound-proofed and darkened, so that both acoustic installations (e.g. the Ursonate, examples of sound poetry, radio plays) as well as a blacked-out room (for 'discovering literature by touch') would be feasible.

[…]

2.4.2 Multimedia Book

Electronic facsimiles can be produced of exhibits that need special protection. The digitally photographed pages of a volume are projected onto a book with white pages. By a relatively simple technical device (bar code or infrared interface) the projector can register when the visitor turns the page and thus select the image of the page in question. In this way an entire book can be exhibited, while in the customary cabinet presentation only the pages at which the book is opened or the binding can be seen.

This form of presentation not only fits in well with our concept based on the book idea; in a museum it also has great educational potential. Technically, image projection need not be restricted to a sequence of stills, it can also include film sequences. In this way, for instance, with appropriate acoustic equipment (headphones, sound-proofing), visitors could take in a presentation and the text of a scene from a play simultaneously.

Another particularly appropriate application is visualization of the genesis of a text. Knowledge of this highly interesting process is usually denied to non-philologists, due to the difficulty of reading historical-critical sources. With projected images the stages of development of a text could be consecutively visualized, the individual transitions illustrated, e.g. by animated appearance or disappearance of sections of manuscript, colouring or deletion of words etc. Analytical studies of texts could also be illustrated in this way, e.g. by visualizing rhythmic structures, semantic isotopies, or intertextual references.

Competition host Schiller Society, Marbach
Project Europe-wide competition for new Museum of German 20th Century Literature within the existing Schillerhöhe in Marbach.

Concept KMS devised the concept for exhibition design and interior planning submitted as part of the entry by an architectural practice in Munich.

Comment The jury selected the London based architect David Chipperfield for the main design. KMS's proposals for the exhibition design and information system were strongly recommended by the jury, and at the time of writing (summer 2002) the possibility of incorporating them into the winning design is being studied.

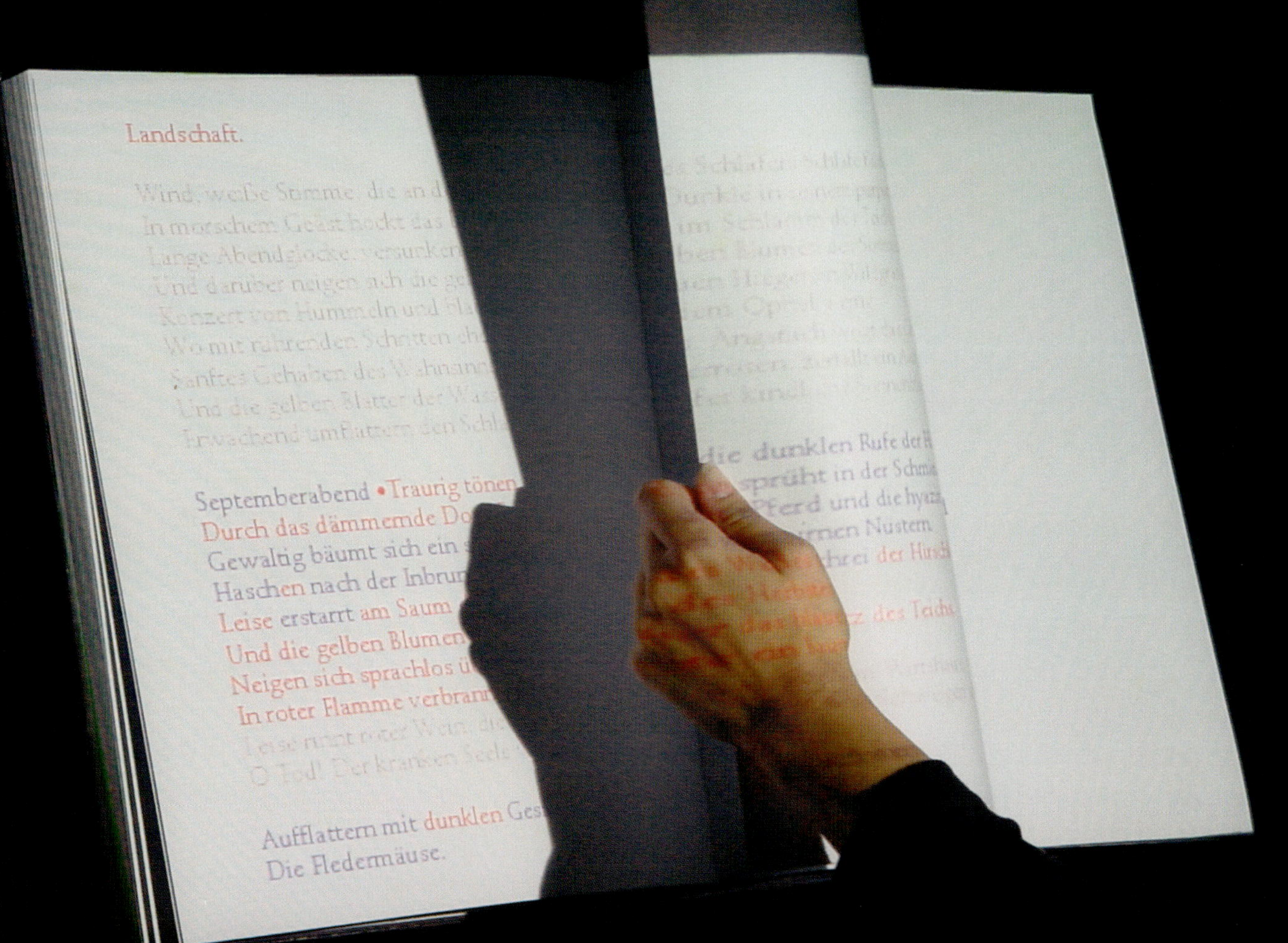

Landschaft.

Wind, weiße Stimme, die an d...
In morschem Geäst hockt das ...
Lange Abendglocke, versunken ...
Und darüber neigen sich die ge...
Konzert von Hummeln und Fla...
Wo mit rührenden Schritten eh...
Sanftes Gehaben des Wahnsinn...
Und die gelben Blätter der Was...
Erwachend umflattern den Schl...

Septemberabend • Traurig tönen ...
Durch das dämmernde Do...
Gewaltig bäumt sich ein ...
Haschen nach der Inbrun...
Leise erstarrt am Saum ...
Und die gelben Blumen ...
Neigen sich sprachlos ü...
In roter Flamme verbrann...
Leise rührt eter Wein, d...
O Tod! Der kranken Seele ...

Aufflattern mit dunklen Ges...
Die Fledermäuse.

"Painting a picture is not a form of self-expression. It is, like any other art, a language by which you communicate about the world."
Mark Rothko

Semantics A vasistas, in French, is a window or opening in a door. The word derives from 'was ist das?' the kind of question a nervous householder or alert sentry might shout through such an opening, in the troubled times of the early 18th century in northern Europe, when monarchical ambitions and religious power combined to redraw the map several times over. By the end of the Seven Years War the word was established in the language, entering France from the north and east, not surprisingly. Languages borrow from each other the whole time. Once 'park' in English meant a pleasant expanse of grass, trees and flowers, now worldwide it designates a slab of tarmac to leave a car on. But vasistas is a kind of transmuted borrowing: a new word for a new phenomenon, not a translation or substitution. As such it is proof of the vitality and depth of which language can be capable.

Successful design needs to have such vitality and depth, and achieves this through using the tools of language, even if they are visual, not verbal. This involves creating a semantic structure — as in architecture the elements articulate the concept, or in a signage system the relations between type sizes and colours establish a hierarchy, that the user can understand.

But even in design solutions without such visible final structures, the designer needs to construct a system of links and signs to bring the whole into a coherent structure. The pages of sketches in a designer's notebook may suggest that the work is only visual, but that would be a superficial reaction. In a successful design the visual has to relate to an ordering of reality through language: there has to be an answer to the question 'what is it?'

Pantone 1797

Pantone 187

HKS 16

Pantone 201

HKS 18

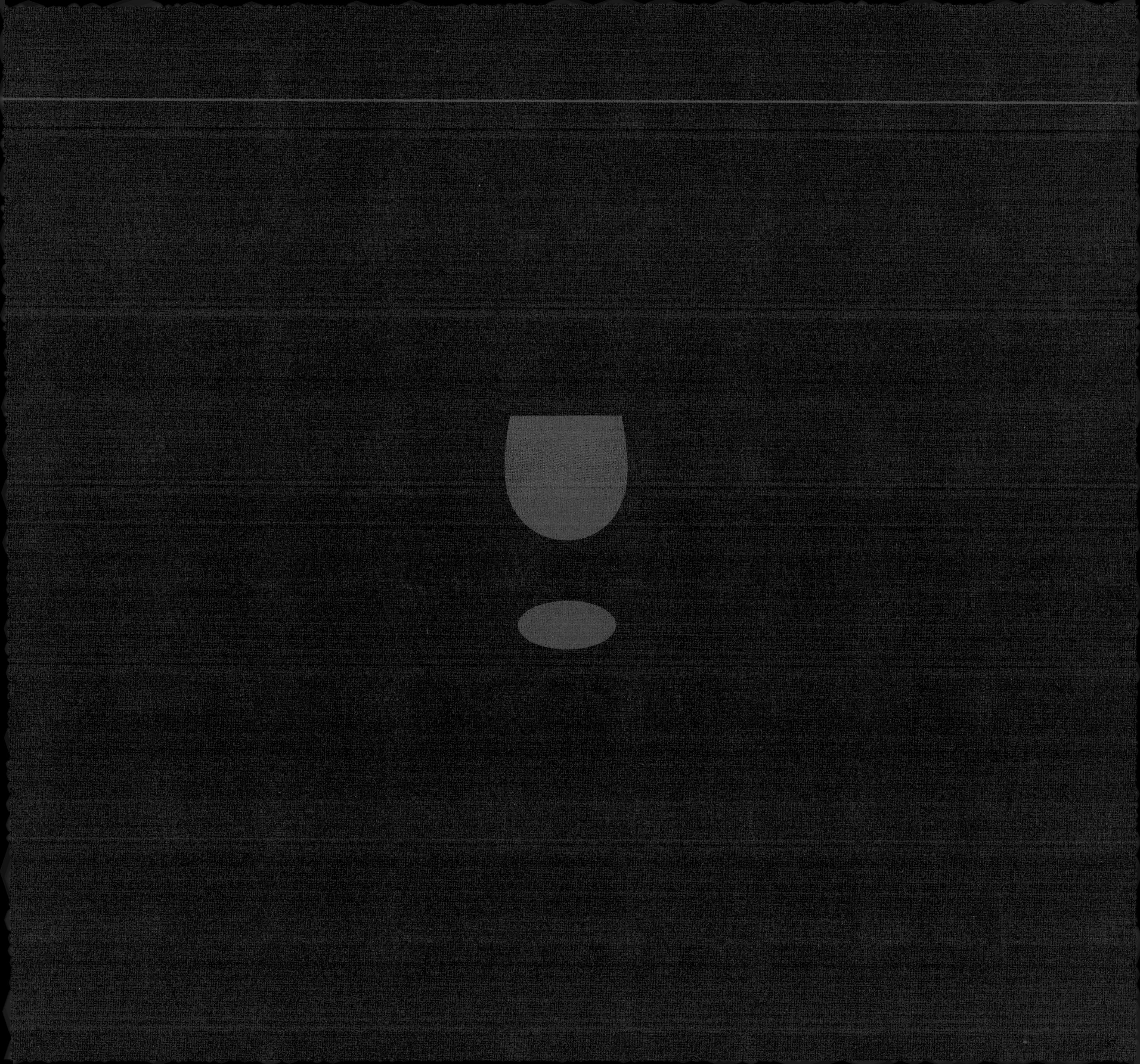

Client Hallwag, Munich
Project Corporate Identity

Brief The client is the leading publisher of books on wine in the German language market. The concept should clearly communicate the central interest of the client, and position it appropriately in the premium sector of the market. The new identity should clearly separate the client's books from the competition, and emphasise their fastidious quality.

Concept At the centre of the new identity is the pictogram, an image based on a glass of wine. This symbolises, in an abstract way, the key competence of the publishing house. The colour range is based on the tones of red wines and evokes their sensual quality.

The mark is also the basis for a systematic design treatment for the books and series published by Hallwag. All cover designs use a frame motif, reminiscent of a wine label, and each series of books has its particular version of the scheme. This explains how titles are related to the frame, the placing of key visual elements, the choice of colour backgrounds and the selection of photography to set the appropriate mood.

Comment All the elements in the new corporate identity for Hallwag derive logically from the definition of the company's role. The pictogram, house colours, and design structure create an immediate link to the core subject of wine, and so make Hallwag's identity and claims unmistakeable. The strapline 'Wein lesen' (reading wine) also plays on the other senses of the two words and can be read as 'gathering grapes'.

Hallwag Wein lesen

"One should not wipe away the zigzags of our journey, because those zigzags are all that is left us."
Stanisław Lem: His Master's Voice

Authenticity 'Anything reticulated or decussated at equal intervals, with interstices between the intersections': this definition of a net may have been seen by its 18th century audience as the amusing pedantry of a 'harmless drudge' (which is how Samuel Johnson described his profession of lexicographer, in his Dictionary of 1755, often identified as the first true dictionary of English). Today, living in a world wired together on a web, we are more disposed to understand the intricacies of an abstract definition of a net: Johnson seems almost prescient. In fact he is simply being authentic, going behind the external appearance of an object into a true account of its nature, which could then be extended to fit new variations of the same concept. His words do not just describe a net but any net, in whatever material – even digital information. Such abstract descriptions allow us to make connexions between objects that seem dissimilar. In the same way as topography shows that, geometrically, a donut is the same kind of object as a teacup: must make breakfast more fun, as well.

Authenticity in design should be equally revelatory. It goes beyond the honesty to materials and purpose that was part of the Modernist creed into being a quest for the necessary truth of a design solution. By defining the role and meaning of each element in a design solution the validity of the whole can be checked, and the semantic structure identified as well. As such, authenticity informs both the process and the result. An authentic solution has to be the result of an authentic process, and so looking for authenticity in a design validates the study of the design process. In this respect most importantly, but in other ways also, to look only at the end results of design limits our understanding of the totality of design. Only by seeing the connexions, and understanding the making, can we unravel the net.

Client Evotec OAI, Hamburg and Oxford
Project Annual report 2001

Brief This was the third annual report KMS had created for the biotech company Evotec (which completed its merger with OAI in 2000). KMS had also created the corporate identity for the new company and so the annual report should reflect this. In addition to including the complete financial information, the report should also show the particular strengths of the company in the field of integrated research and development of biotechnology products. Thus Evotec OAI's activities in the complex field of biotechnology would be made clearer.

Concept The different stages and activities in the research process and in the development of new products should be explained visually, but not at all by conventional photo-documentation. Individuals working in the company were sent single-use cameras and asked to make a personal and informal record of their work and workplace. This produced some 500 images from which the designers made a selection to show, as a complete process of integrated drug discovery and development, the different activities of the company. The result is a photographic narrative covering eight consecutive double-page spreads, which is in turn the main structural element in the overall report. The cover shows the organisational and functional structure of the company as an abstract graphic.

Comments Looking at the actual work of the company made the annual report a more authentic and credible document, and the approach was welcomed by the company's employees who were able to identify with the result more closely.

evotec OAI
1
evotec OAI
7
HIT PROFILING
HH
evotec OAI
13
CHEMINFORMATICS   NOV 2001
Oxford
evotec OAI
19
Gerion   8.11.01
Ulrike Bischoff
Katja Alm
Heike Dassmann
Anke Schönborn
Andreas Ebneth
HH   Hendrik Bothmann
evotec OAI
2
Hamburg
evotec OAI
8
8.11.2001   EVOTEC OAI
Labelling Chemistry
HH
evotec OAI
14
PRD   6-8 NOV
John Knight
Ox
evotec OAI
20
Assay Development I   12.11.01
II   20.12.01
Karen
HH
evotec OAI
3
Labelling Chemistry   04.10.2001
ST   05.11.2001
HH Profiling   15.10.2001
Hamburg
evotec OAI
9
Screening Operations   07.11.01
Screening Service
Julian Wells
HH
evotec OAI
15
Commercial + admin   Nov 01
OXFORD
Adrienne J. Murray
evotec OAI
21
ENS (Target Discovery)
HH
evotec OAI
4
Pan-MERC Development
MERC ASSOC: DISCOVERY
Ox
evotec OAI
10
DISCOVERY CHEMISTRY   17/12/01
Ox
evotec OAI
16
Jon Cook.
Analytical.
OXFORD
evotec OAI
5
Logistics (Gebäude)   05.11
HH
evotec OAI
11
Quality / Reg. Support
Ox
evotec OAI
17
RON SCOTT
PILOT PLANTS
OXFORD
evotec OAI
23
CHEMINFORMATICS II   Nov 2001
Oxford
Maurice Ellimay
A. Hammer
evotec OAI
6
Elektronik /
Optik
R. Gange   HH
evotec OAI
12
Custom preps -
Development
Chemistry
OXFORD
Petra Diutrich
evotec OAI
18
Admin, Quality, Commercial,
HR
Ox
evotec OAI
24
ENS II
HH

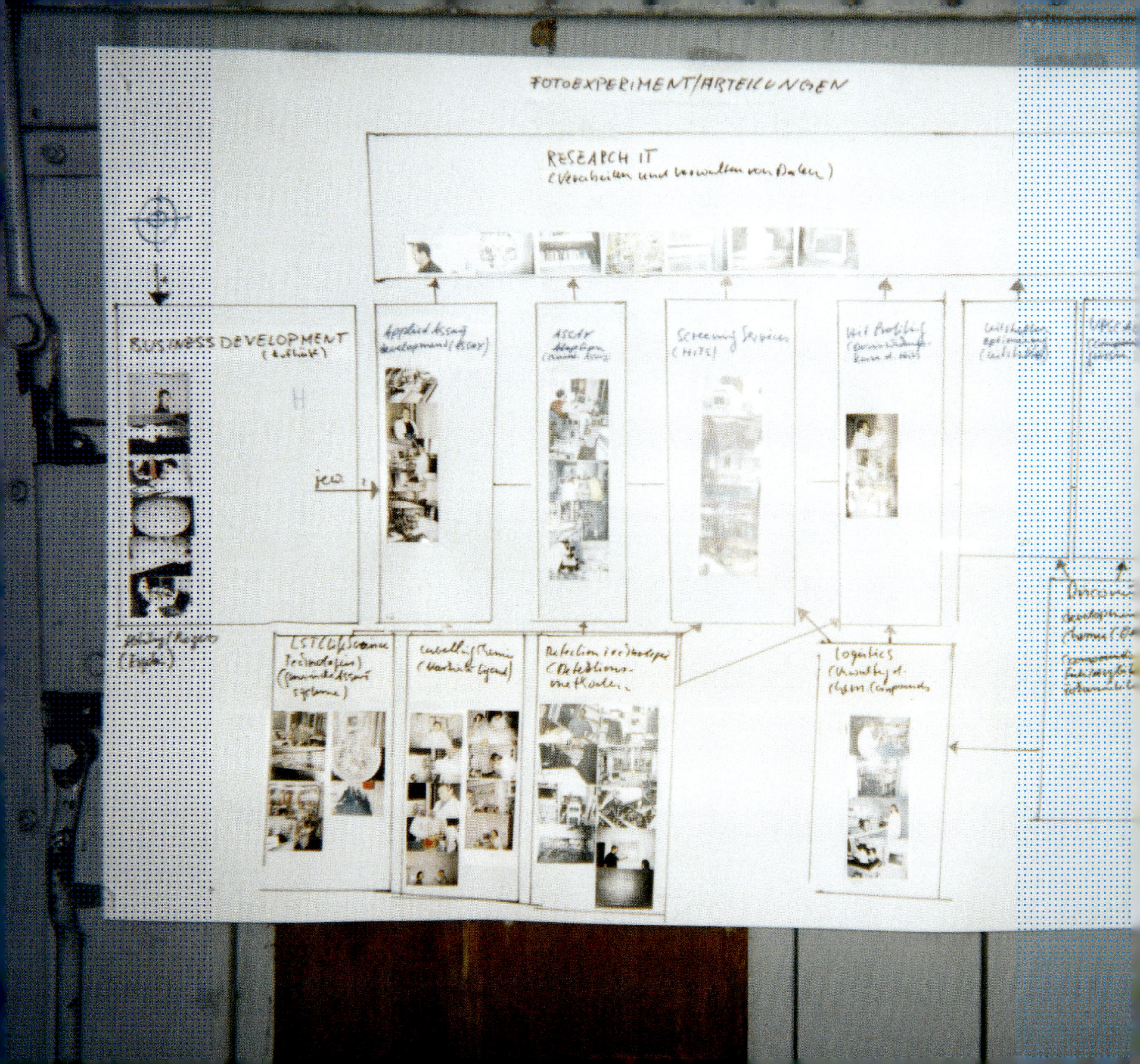

FOTOEXPERIMENT/ABTEILUNGEN

RESEARCH IT
(Verarbeiten und verwalten von Daten)

BUSINESS DEVELOPMENT
(Aufbau)

jew.

Applied Assay
development (ASSAY)

ASSAY
Adaptation
(Routine Assay)

Screening Services
(HITS)

Hit Profiling
(Darreichung,
Kenn. d. Hits)

Leitstruktur
optimierung
(Leitstruktur)

LST (Life Science
Technologien)
(Sammelassay
systeme)

Labelling Chemie
(Markierte Ligand)

Detection technologie
(Detections-
methoden)

Logistics
(Verwaltung d.
Chem. Compounds)

011A: 2st.eps
013A: 21.10.80
015A: 24.eps

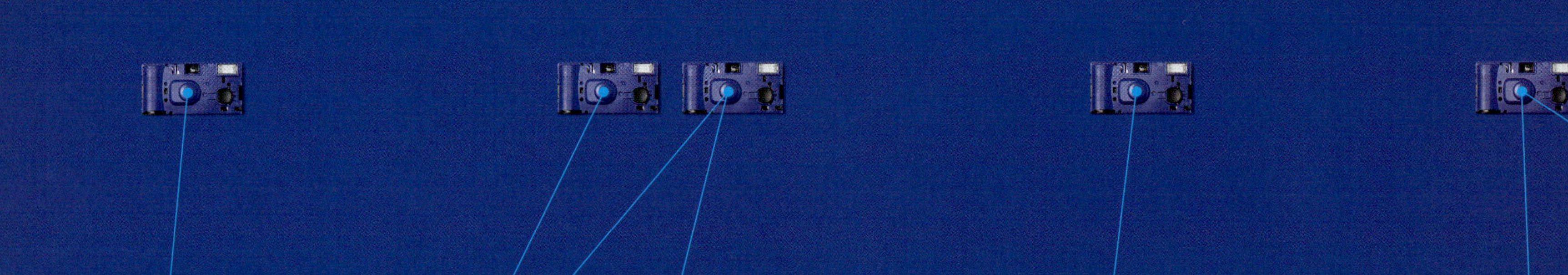
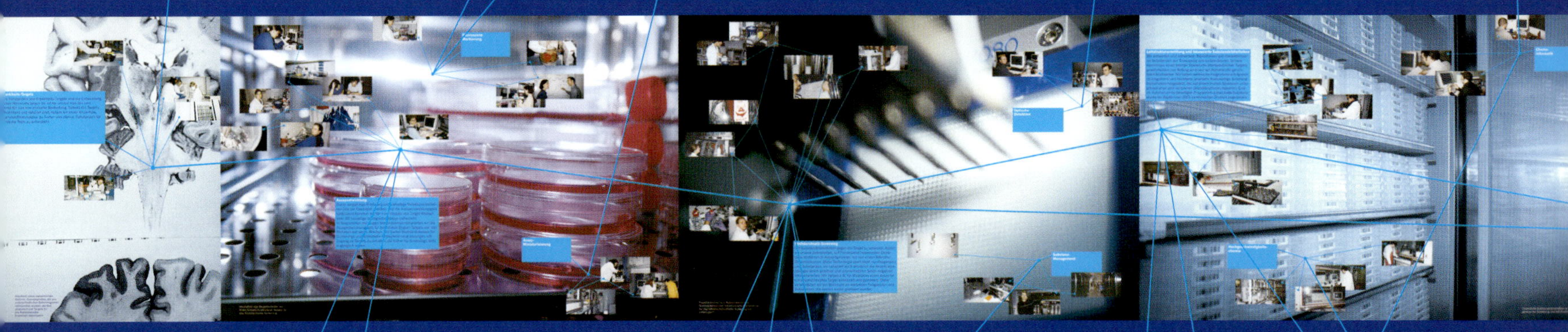

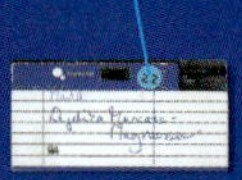

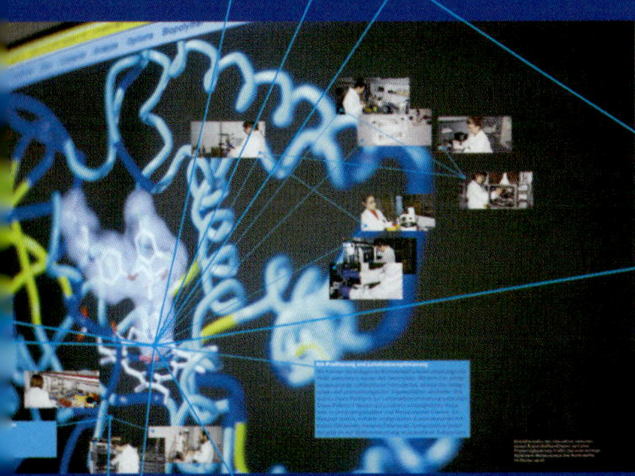
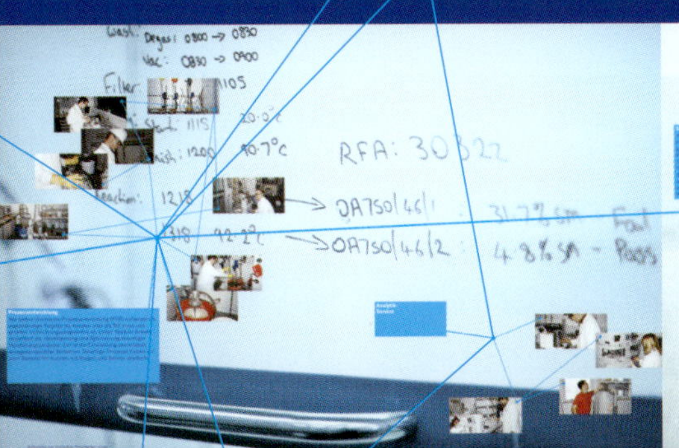

Wash: Dryer: 0800 → 0850
Vac: 0810 → 0900
Filter: 1105
Std: 1115
RH: 1200   10.7°C
RFA: 30322
→ OA750/46/1
→ OA750/46/2   4.8% SA — Pass

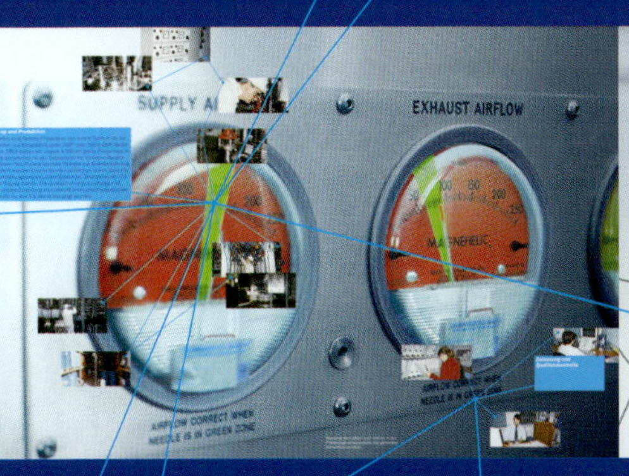

SUPPLY AIRFLOW
EXHAUST AIRFLOW
MAGNEHELIC
AIRFLOW CORRECT WHEN
NEEDLE IS IN GREEN ZONE

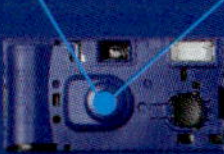

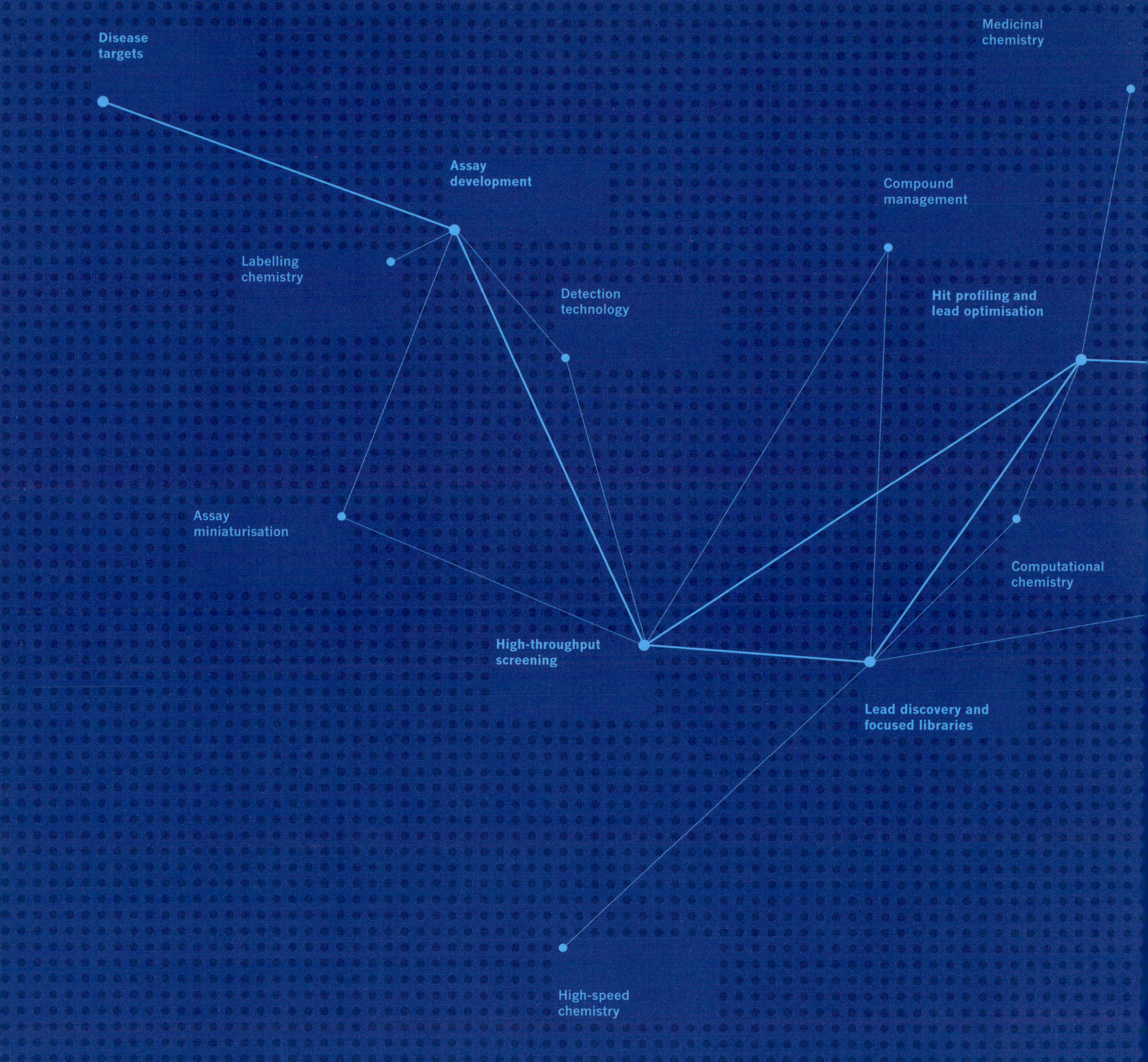

Disease targets
Medicinal chemistry
Assay development
Compound management
Labelling chemistry
Detection technology
Hit profiling and lead optimisation
Assay miniaturisation
Computational chemistry
High-throughput screening
Lead discovery and focused libraries
High-speed chemistry

Process research
and development
Scale-up
and manufacture
Analytical
services
Regulatory and
quality support
IND | New drug

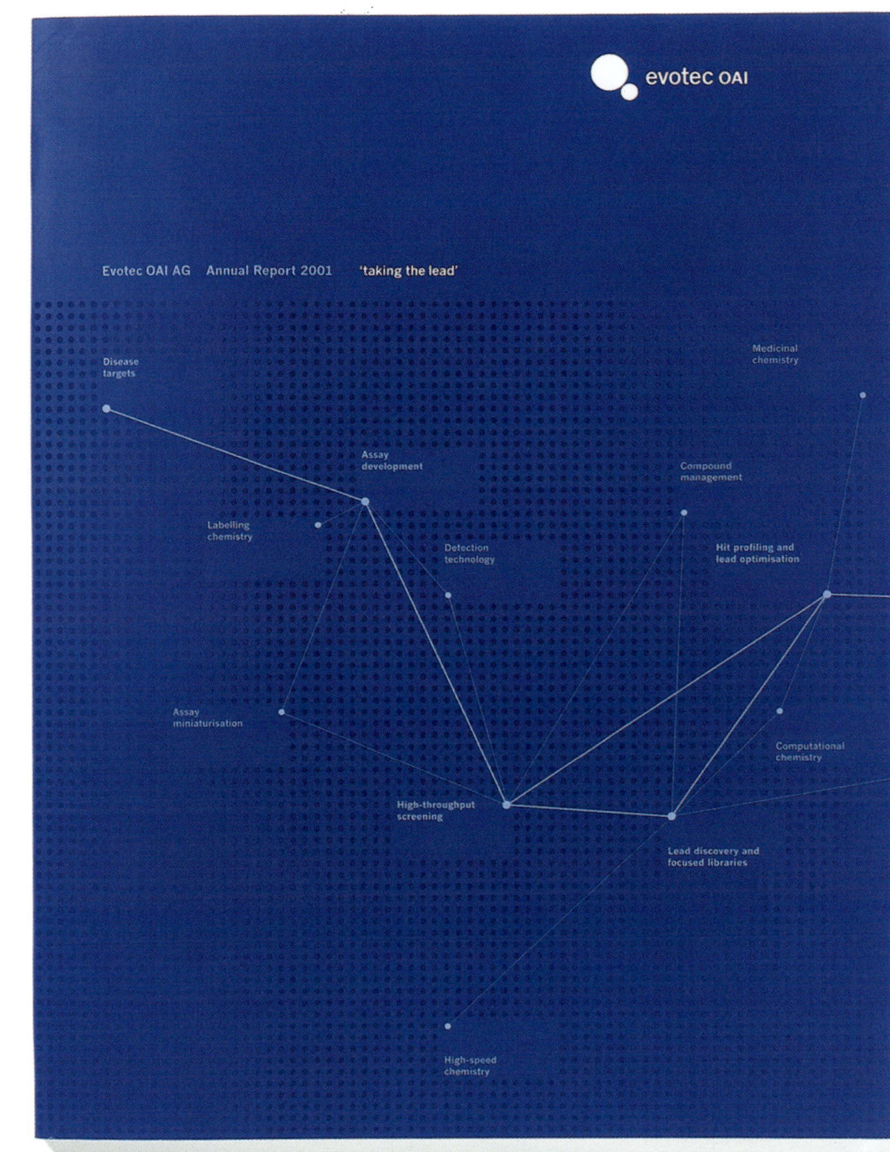

evotec OAI
Evotec OAI AG   Annual Report 2001   'taking the lead'
Disease targets
Medicinal chemistry
Assay development
Compound management
Labelling chemistry
Detection technology
Hit profiling and lead optimisation
Assay miniaturisation
Computational chemistry
High-throughput screening
Lead discovery and focused libraries
High-speed chemistry

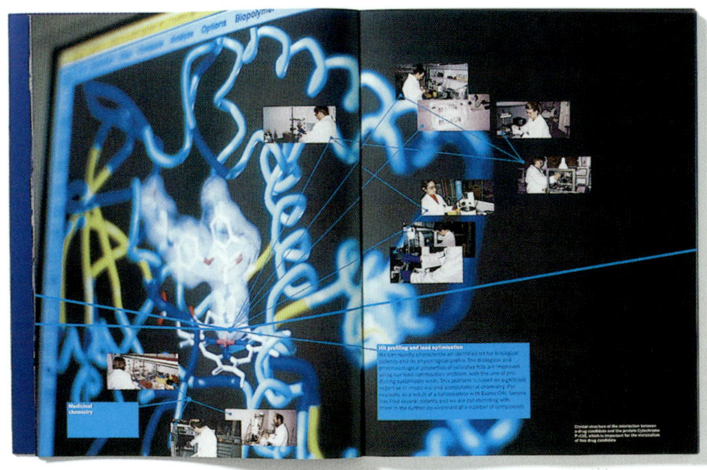

Crystal structure of the interaction between a drug candidate and the protein Cytochrome P-450, which is important for the metabolism of this drug candidate

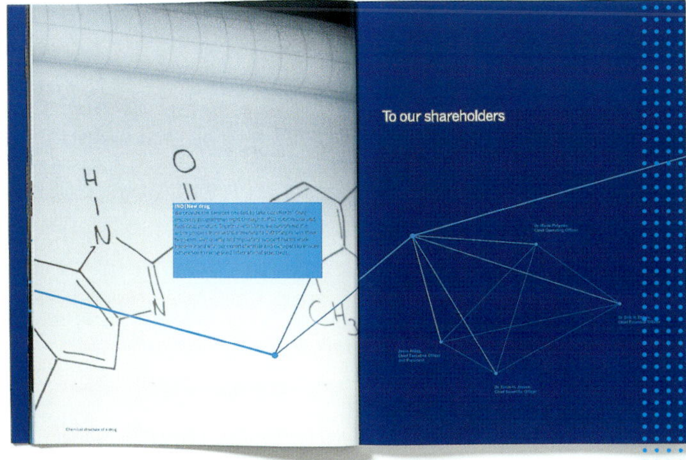

Chemical structure of a drug

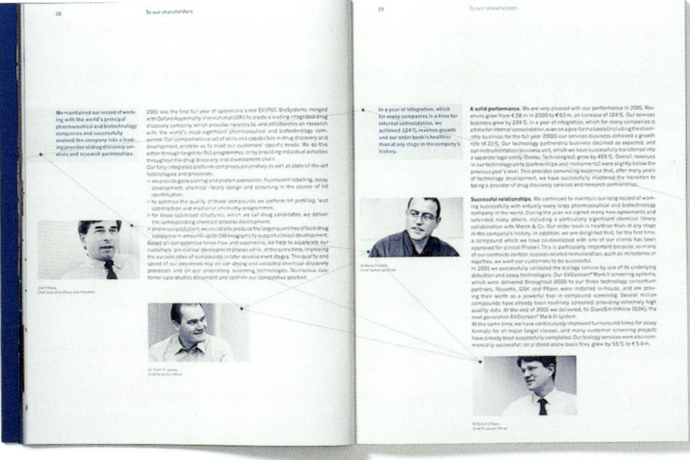

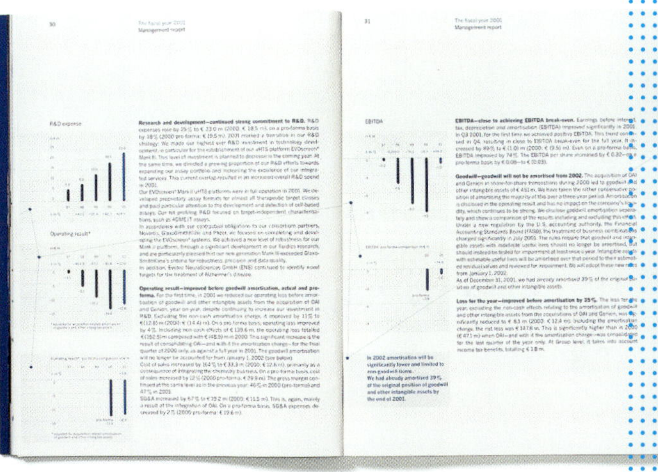

Identity

Visitor to a natural history museum: "What's that bird?"
Friend: "It's a guillemot."
Visitor: "That's not my idea of a guillemot."
Friend: "No, dear, it's Nature's idea of a guillemot…"

Identity Our experience tells us, as it did the 18th century Irish philosopher Berkeley, that 'esse est percipi' — observation predicates existence. Today, shorn of the metaphysics, the phrase reads like the strapline for a mediated age. Football heroes and fashion models, short-term politicians and soap opera stars only live, it seems, as long as they are lit by the paparazzi's flashguns. Image-conscious corporations, too, make themselves over at regular intervals, as if without the reminders clients and shareholders might forget who they were.

But the issue of identity, pace Berkeley, is more than a matter of surface impressions, even though impressions may be all we have to go on. We know that our own personal identities are a melange of our physical appearance (about which the mirror deceives us every morning) with our attributes, ideas, opinions and attitudes, some of which are made visible through our behaviour. We define the identities of others through a similar mixture of visual and non-visual, direct and indirect information.

The task for a designer dealing with an identity, whether for a rock band or a realtor, is firstly to decide what to make visible — or what in the ethos, experience or expectations of a client can be made visible, but then to find an abstract form, through colour and content, that will communicate that vision successfully. This is a job that requires both imagination and analysis, and depends for its success on enunciating the different elements in a coherent and compelling way. The whole has to be consistent within itself and present a meaningful image to the outside world. In this sense an identity is not something created by the designer but something whose existence the designer makes evident. The only test of success is whether the design is seen to work (just as Berkeley's somewhat extreme conclusion was that the only proof of anything's existence was our subjective knowledge of it.)

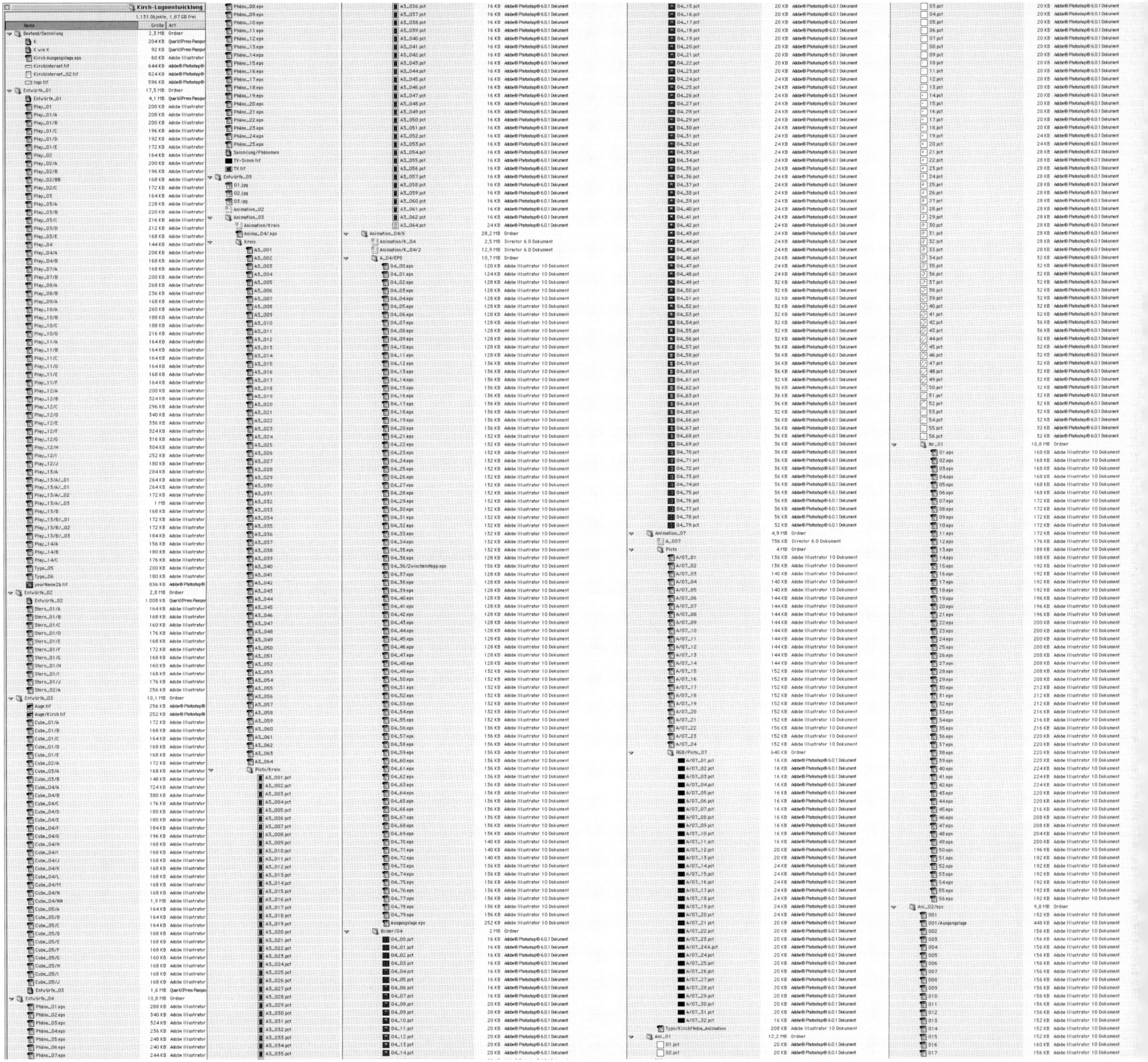

Kirch-Logoentwicklung

1.131 Objekte, 1,87 GB frei

Name	Größe	Art
▽ Bestand/Sammlung	2,3 MB	Ordner
K	204 KB	QuarkXPress Passport
K wie K	92 KB	QuarkXPress Passport
Kirch Ausgangslage.eps	60 KB	Adobe Illustrator
KirchInternet.tif	644 KB	Adobe® Photoshop®
KirchInternet_02.tif	824 KB	Adobe® Photoshop®
logo.tif	596 KB	Adobe® Photoshop®
▽ Entwürfe_01	17,5 MB	Ordner
Entwürfe_01	4,1 MB	QuarkXPress Passport
Play_01	200 KB	Adobe Illustrator
Play_01/A	208 KB	Adobe Illustrator
Play_01/B	200 KB	Adobe Illustrator
Play_01/C	196 KB	Adobe Illustrator
Play_01/D	192 KB	Adobe Illustrator
Play_01/E	172 KB	Adobe Illustrator
Play_02	164 KB	Adobe Illustrator
Play_02/A	200 KB	Adobe Illustrator
Play_02/B	196 KB	Adobe Illustrator
Play_02/BB	168 KB	Adobe Illustrator
Play_02/C	172 KB	Adobe Illustrator
Play_03	164 KB	Adobe Illustrator
Play_03/A	228 KB	Adobe Illustrator
Play_03/B	220 KB	Adobe Illustrator
Play_03/C	216 KB	Adobe Illustrator
Play_03/D	212 KB	Adobe Illustrator
Play_03/E	168 KB	Adobe Illustrator
Play_04	144 KB	Adobe Illustrator
Play_04/A	208 KB	Adobe Illustrator
Play_04/B	160 KB	Adobe Illustrator
Play_07/A	264 KB	Adobe Illustrator
Play_07/B	200 KB	Adobe Illustrator
Play_08/A	268 KB	Adobe Illustrator
Play_08/B	236 KB	Adobe Illustrator
Play_09/A	168 KB	Adobe Illustrator
Play_10/A	260 KB	Adobe Illustrator
Play_10/B	168 KB	Adobe Illustrator
Play_10/C	188 KB	Adobe Illustrator
Play_10/D	216 KB	Adobe Illustrator
Play_11/A	164 KB	Adobe Illustrator
Play_11/B	164 KB	Adobe Illustrator
Play_11/C	164 KB	Adobe Illustrator
Play_11/D	164 KB	Adobe Illustrator
Play_11/E	168 KB	Adobe Illustrator
Play_11/F	164 KB	Adobe Illustrator
Play_12/A	200 KB	Adobe Illustrator
Play_12/B	324 KB	Adobe Illustrator
Play_12/C	296 KB	Adobe Illustrator
Play_12/D	340 KB	Adobe Illustrator
Play_12/E	336 KB	Adobe Illustrator
Play_12/F	324 KB	Adobe Illustrator
Play_12/G	316 KB	Adobe Illustrator
Play_12/H	304 KB	Adobe Illustrator
Play_12/I	252 KB	Adobe Illustrator
Play_12/J	180 KB	Adobe Illustrator
Play_13/A	284 KB	Adobe Illustrator
Play_13/A/_01	264 KB	Adobe Illustrator
Play_13/A/_01	264 KB	Adobe Illustrator
Play_13/A/_02	172 KB	Adobe Illustrator
Play_13/A/_03	1 MB	Adobe Illustrator
Play_13/B	168 KB	Adobe Illustrator
Play_13/B/_01	172 KB	Adobe Illustrator
Play_13/B/_02	172 KB	Adobe Illustrator
Play_13/B/_03	168 KB	Adobe Illustrator
Play_14/A	156 KB	Adobe Illustrator
Play_14/B	176 KB	Adobe Illustrator
Play_14/C	176 KB	Adobe Illustrator
Typo_05	200 KB	Adobe Illustrator
Typo_06	180 KB	Adobe Illustrator
yourName2b.tif	836 KB	Adobe® Photoshop®
▽ Entwürfe_02	2,8 MB	Ordner
Entwürfe_02	1.008 KB	QuarkXPress Passport
Stern_01/A	164 KB	Adobe Illustrator
Stern_01/B	168 KB	Adobe Illustrator
Stern_01/C	160 KB	Adobe Illustrator
Stern_01/D	176 KB	Adobe Illustrator
Stern_01/E	168 KB	Adobe Illustrator
Stern_01/F	172 KB	Adobe Illustrator
Stern_01/F	168 KB	Adobe Illustrator
Stern_01/G	168 KB	Adobe Illustrator
Stern_01/H	160 KB	Adobe Illustrator
Stern_01/I	168 KB	Adobe Illustrator
Stern_01/J	176 KB	Adobe Illustrator
Stern_02/A	256 KB	Adobe Illustrator
▽ Entwürfe_03	10,1 MB	Ordner
Auge.tif	256 KB	Adobe® Photoshop®
Auge/Kirch.tif	252 KB	Adobe® Photoshop®
Cube_01/A	172 KB	Adobe Illustrator
Cube_01/B	168 KB	Adobe Illustrator
Cube_01/C	164 KB	Adobe Illustrator
Cube_01/D	168 KB	Adobe Illustrator
Cube_01/E	168 KB	Adobe Illustrator
Cube_02/A	172 KB	Adobe Illustrator
Cube_03/A	168 KB	Adobe Illustrator
Cube_03/B	148 KB	Adobe Illustrator
Cube_04/A	724 KB	Adobe Illustrator
Cube_04/B	380 KB	Adobe Illustrator
Cube_04/C	176 KB	Adobe Illustrator
Cube_04/D	180 KB	Adobe Illustrator
Cube_04/E	168 KB	Adobe Illustrator
Cube_04/F	184 KB	Adobe Illustrator
Cube_04/G	196 KB	Adobe Illustrator
Cube_04/H	168 KB	Adobe Illustrator
Cube_04/I	168 KB	Adobe Illustrator
Cube_04/J	160 KB	Adobe Illustrator
Cube_04/K	168 KB	Adobe Illustrator
Cube_04/L	168 KB	Adobe Illustrator
Cube_04/M	168 KB	Adobe Illustrator
Cube_04/N	168 KB	Adobe Illustrator
Cube_04/NN	1,9 MB	Adobe Illustrator
Cube_05/A	164 KB	Adobe Illustrator
Cube_05/B	164 KB	Adobe Illustrator
Cube_05/C	164 KB	Adobe Illustrator
Cube_05/D	168 KB	Adobe Illustrator
Cube_05/E	168 KB	Adobe Illustrator
Cube_05/F	168 KB	Adobe Illustrator
Cube_05/G	160 KB	Adobe Illustrator
Cube_05/H	168 KB	Adobe Illustrator
Cube_05/I	168 KB	Adobe Illustrator
Cube_05/J	168 KB	Adobe Illustrator
Entwürfe_03	1,6 MB	QuarkXPress Passport
▽ Entwürfe_04	10,8 MB	Ordner
Phäno_01.eps	288 KB	Adobe Illustrator
Phäno_02.eps	340 KB	Adobe Illustrator
Phäno_03.eps	324 KB	Adobe Illustrator
Phäno_04.eps	236 KB	Adobe Illustrator
Phäno_05.eps	248 KB	Adobe Illustrator
Phäno_06.eps	240 KB	Adobe Illustrator
Phäno_07.eps	244 KB	Adobe Illustrator

Name	Size	Kind
018	156 KB	Adobe Illustrator 10 Dokument
019	152 KB	Adobe Illustrator 10 Dokument
020	156 KB	Adobe Illustrator 10 Dokument
021	152 KB	Adobe Illustrator 10 Dokument
022	152 KB	Adobe Illustrator 10 Dokument
023	152 KB	Adobe Illustrator 10 Dokument
024	152 KB	Adobe Illustrator 10 Dokument
025	152 KB	Adobe Illustrator 10 Dokument
026	152 KB	Adobe Illustrator 10 Dokument
027	152 KB	Adobe Illustrator 10 Dokument
028	152 KB	Adobe Illustrator 10 Dokument
029	152 KB	Adobe Illustrator 10 Dokument
030	152 KB	Adobe Illustrator 10 Dokument
031	152 KB	Adobe Illustrator 10 Dokument
032	152 KB	Adobe Illustrator 10 Dokument
033	152 KB	Adobe Illustrator 10 Dokument
034	152 KB	Adobe Illustrator 10 Dokument
035	148 KB	Adobe Illustrator 10 Dokument
036	152 KB	Adobe Illustrator 10 Dokument
037	152 KB	Adobe Illustrator 10 Dokument
038	152 KB	Adobe Illustrator 10 Dokument
039	152 KB	Adobe Illustrator 10 Dokument
040	152 KB	Adobe Illustrator 10 Dokument
041	152 KB	Adobe Illustrator 10 Dokument
042	152 KB	Adobe Illustrator 10 Dokument
043-50	152 KB	Adobe Illustrator 10 Dokument
044	152 KB	Adobe Illustrator 10 Dokument
045	152 KB	Adobe Illustrator 10 Dokument
046	152 KB	Adobe Illustrator 10 Dokument
047	152 KB	Adobe Illustrator 10 Dokument
048	152 KB	Adobe Illustrator 10 Dokument
048/Last	200 KB	Adobe Illustrator 10 Dokument
051	152 KB	Adobe Illustrator 10 Dokument
052	148 KB	Adobe Illustrator 10 Dokument
053	152 KB	Adobe Illustrator 10 Dokument
054	152 KB	Adobe Illustrator 10 Dokument
055	152 KB	Adobe Illustrator 10 Dokument
056	152 KB	Adobe Illustrator 10 Dokument
057	152 KB	Adobe Illustrator 10 Dokument
058	152 KB	Adobe Illustrator 10 Dokument
059	152 KB	Adobe Illustrator 10 Dokument
060	152 KB	Adobe Illustrator 10 Dokument
061	148 KB	Adobe Illustrator 10 Dokument
062	148 KB	Adobe Illustrator 10 Dokument
063/end	148 KB	Adobe Illustrator 10 Dokument
Auge- und Phäno.eps	180 KB	Adobe Illustrator 10 Dokument
Picts/Ani_02	1,4 MB	Ordner
001.pct	20 KB	Adobe Photoshop 6.0.1 Dokument
002.pct	20 KB	Adobe Photoshop 6.0.1 Dokument
003.pct	20 KB	Adobe Photoshop 6.0.1 Dokument
004.pct	20 KB	Adobe Photoshop 6.0.1 Dokument
005.pct	20 KB	Adobe Photoshop 6.0.1 Dokument
006.pct	20 KB	Adobe Photoshop 6.0.1 Dokument
007.pct	20 KB	Adobe Photoshop 6.0.1 Dokument
008.pct	20 KB	Adobe Photoshop 6.0.1 Dokument
009.pct	20 KB	Adobe Photoshop 6.0.1 Dokument
010.pct	20 KB	Adobe Photoshop 6.0.1 Dokument
011.pct	20 KB	Adobe Photoshop 6.0.1 Dokument
012.pct	20 KB	Adobe Photoshop 6.0.1 Dokument
013.pct	20 KB	Adobe Photoshop 6.0.1 Dokument
014.pct	20 KB	Adobe Photoshop 6.0.1 Dokument
015.pct	20 KB	Adobe Photoshop 6.0.1 Dokument
016.pct	20 KB	Adobe Photoshop 6.0.1 Dokument
017.pct	20 KB	Adobe Photoshop 6.0.1 Dokument
018.pct	20 KB	Adobe Photoshop 6.0.1 Dokument
019.pct	20 KB	Adobe Photoshop 6.0.1 Dokument
020.pct	20 KB	Adobe Photoshop 6.0.1 Dokument
021.pct	20 KB	Adobe Photoshop 6.0.1 Dokument
022.pct	16 KB	Adobe Photoshop 6.0.1 Dokument
023.pct	20 KB	Adobe Photoshop 6.0.1 Dokument
024.pct	20 KB	Adobe Photoshop 6.0.1 Dokument
025.pct	20 KB	Adobe Photoshop 6.0.1 Dokument
026.pct	20 KB	Adobe Photoshop 6.0.1 Dokument
027.pct	20 KB	Adobe Photoshop 6.0.1 Dokument
028.pct	20 KB	Adobe Photoshop 6.0.1 Dokument
029.pct	20 KB	Adobe Photoshop 6.0.1 Dokument
030.pct	20 KB	Adobe Photoshop 6.0.1 Dokument
031.pct	20 KB	Adobe Photoshop 6.0.1 Dokument
032.pct	20 KB	Adobe Photoshop 6.0.1 Dokument
033.pct	20 KB	Adobe Photoshop 6.0.1 Dokument
034.pct	20 KB	Adobe Photoshop 6.0.1 Dokument
035.pct	20 KB	Adobe Photoshop 6.0.1 Dokument
036.pct	20 KB	Adobe Photoshop 6.0.1 Dokument
037.pct	20 KB	Adobe Photoshop 6.0.1 Dokument
038.pct	20 KB	Adobe Photoshop 6.0.1 Dokument
039.pct	20 KB	Adobe Photoshop 6.0.1 Dokument
040.pct	20 KB	Adobe Photoshop 6.0.1 Dokument
041.pct	20 KB	Adobe Photoshop 6.0.1 Dokument
042.pct	20 KB	Adobe Photoshop 6.0.1 Dokument
043-50.pct	20 KB	Adobe Photoshop 6.0.1 Dokument
043.pct	20 KB	Adobe Photoshop 6.0.1 Dokument
044.pct	20 KB	Adobe Photoshop 6.0.1 Dokument
045.pct	20 KB	Adobe Photoshop 6.0.1 Dokument
046.pct	20 KB	Adobe Photoshop 6.0.1 Dokument
047.pct	20 KB	Adobe Photoshop 6.0.1 Dokument
048.pct	20 KB	Adobe Photoshop 6.0.1 Dokument
051.pct	20 KB	Adobe Photoshop 6.0.1 Dokument
052.pct	20 KB	Adobe Photoshop 6.0.1 Dokument
053.pct	20 KB	Adobe Photoshop 6.0.1 Dokument
054.pct	20 KB	Adobe Photoshop 6.0.1 Dokument
055.pct	20 KB	Adobe Photoshop 6.0.1 Dokument
056.pct	20 KB	Adobe Photoshop 6.0.1 Dokument
057.pct	20 KB	Adobe Photoshop 6.0.1 Dokument
058.pct	20 KB	Adobe Photoshop 6.0.1 Dokument
059.pct	20 KB	Adobe Photoshop 6.0.1 Dokument
060.pct	20 KB	Adobe Photoshop 6.0.1 Dokument
061.pct	20 KB	Adobe Photoshop 6.0.1 Dokument
062.pct	20 KB	Adobe Photoshop 6.0.1 Dokument
062/A.pct	20 KB	Adobe Photoshop 6.0.1 Dokument
062/B.pct	24 KB	Adobe Photoshop 6.0.1 Dokument
062/C.pct	24 KB	Adobe Photoshop 6.0.1 Dokument
062/D.pct	24 KB	Adobe Photoshop 6.0.1 Dokument
062/F.pct	24 KB	Adobe Photoshop 6.0.1 Dokument
062/G.pct	24 KB	Adobe Photoshop 6.0.1 Dokument
062/H.pct	24 KB	Adobe Photoshop 6.0.1 Dokument
062/I.pct	24 KB	Adobe Photoshop 6.0.1 Dokument
062/J.pct	24 KB	Adobe Photoshop 6.0.1 Dokument
062/K.pct	24 KB	Adobe Photoshop 6.0.1 Dokument
062/L.pct	24 KB	Adobe Photoshop 6.0.1 Dokument
063/end.pct	20 KB	Adobe Photoshop 6.0.1 Dokument
GB_01.eps	172 KB	Adobe Illustrator 10 Dokument
GB_02.eps	172 KB	Adobe Illustrator 10 Dokument
GB_03.eps	168 KB	Adobe Illustrator 10 Dokument
GB_04.eps	176 KB	Adobe Illustrator 10 Dokument
GB_05.eps	176 KB	Adobe Illustrator 10 Dokument
GB_06.eps	172 KB	Adobe Illustrator 10 Dokument
GB_07.eps	180 KB	Adobe Illustrator 10 Dokument
GB_08.eps	168 KB	Adobe Illustrator 10 Dokument

Name	Size	Kind
RGB_09.eps	168 KB	Adobe Illustrator 10 Dokument
RGB_10.eps	164 KB	Adobe Illustrator 10 Dokument
RGB_11.eps	168 KB	Adobe Illustrator 10 Dokument
Sammlung/Animation	28 KB	QuarkXPress Passport™ Dokument
Sammlung/Animationen	1,7 MB	QuarkXPress Passport™ Dokument
Entwürfe_06	6,8 MB	Ordner
Sammlung/system	1,4 MB	QuarkXPress Passport™ Dokument
System_01.eps	188 KB	Adobe Illustrator 10 Dokument
System_02.eps	196 KB	Adobe Illustrator 10 Dokument
System_03.eps	196 KB	Adobe Illustrator 10 Dokument
System_04.eps	188 KB	Adobe Illustrator 10 Dokument
System_05.eps	180 KB	Adobe Illustrator 10 Dokument
System_06.eps	180 KB	Adobe Illustrator 10 Dokument
System_07.eps	176 KB	Adobe Illustrator 10 Dokument
System_08.eps	176 KB	Adobe Illustrator 10 Dokument
System_09.eps	176 KB	Adobe Illustrator 10 Dokument
System_10.eps	176 KB	Adobe Illustrator 10 Dokument
System_11.eps	176 KB	Adobe Illustrator 10 Dokument
Typo/KirchMedia	304 KB	Adobe Illustrator 10 Dokument
Typo/KirchMedia_01	208 KB	Adobe Illustrator 10 Dokument
Typo/KirchMedia_02	196 KB	Adobe Illustrator 10 Dokument
Typo/KirchMedia_03	192 KB	Adobe Illustrator 10 Dokument
Typo/KirchMedia_04	176 KB	Adobe Illustrator 10 Dokument
Typo/KirchMedia_05	184 KB	Adobe Illustrator 10 Dokument
Typo/KirchMedia_06	208 KB	Adobe Illustrator 10 Dokument
Typo/KirchMedia_07	264 KB	Adobe Illustrator 10 Dokument
Typo/KirchMedia_08	208 KB	Adobe Illustrator 10 Dokument
Typo/KirchMedia_09	244 KB	Adobe Illustrator 10 Dokument
Typo/KirchMedia_10	244 KB	Adobe Illustrator 10 Dokument
Typo/KirchMedia_11	208 KB	Adobe Illustrator 10 Dokument
Typo/KirchMedia_12	204 KB	Adobe Illustrator 10 Dokument
Typo/KirchMedia_13	296 KB	Adobe Illustrator 10 Dokument
Typo/KirchMedia_14	316 KB	Adobe Illustrator 10 Dokument
Entwürfe_07	9,8 MB	Ordner
Logotyp	1,5 MB	QuarkXPress Passport™ Dokument
Logotype_01.eps	340 KB	Adobe Illustrator 10 Dokument
Logotype_01/NewsG_01.eps	340 KB	Adobe Illustrator 10 Dokument
Logotype_01/NewsG_02.eps	240 KB	Adobe Illustrator 10 Dokument
Logotype_01/NewsG_03.eps	240 KB	Adobe Illustrator 10 Dokument
Logotype_01/NewsG_04.eps	244 KB	Adobe Illustrator 10 Dokument
Logotype_01/NewsG_05.eps	244 KB	Adobe Illustrator 10 Dokument
Logotype_01/NewsG_06.eps	244 KB	Adobe Illustrator 10 Dokument
Logotype_01/NewsG_07.eps	240 KB	Adobe Illustrator 10 Dokument
Logotype_01/NewsG_08.eps	236 KB	Adobe Illustrator 10 Dokument
Logotype_01/NewsG_09.eps	284 KB	Adobe Illustrator 10 Dokument
Logotype_01/NewsG_10.eps	240 KB	Adobe Illustrator 10 Dokument
Logotype_01/NewsG_11.eps	244 KB	Adobe Illustrator 10 Dokument
Logotype_01/NewsG_12.eps	256 KB	Adobe Illustrator 10 Dokument
Logotype_02/ITC-F_01.eps	360 KB	Adobe Illustrator 10 Dokument
Logotype_02/ITC-F_02.eps	248 KB	Adobe Illustrator 10 Dokument
Logotype_02/ITC-F_03.eps	256 KB	Adobe Illustrator 10 Dokument
Logotype_02/ITC-F_04.eps	296 KB	Adobe Illustrator 10 Dokument
Logotype_02/ITC-F_05.eps	300 KB	Adobe Illustrator 10 Dokument
Logotype_03/01.eps	248 KB	Adobe Illustrator 10 Dokument
Logotype_03/02.eps	356 KB	Adobe Illustrator 10 Dokument
Logotype_03/03.eps	356 KB	Adobe Illustrator 10 Dokument
Logotype_03/04.eps	352 KB	Adobe Illustrator 10 Dokument
Logotype_03/05.eps	356 KB	Adobe Illustrator 10 Dokument
Logotype_04/01.eps	332 KB	Adobe Illustrator 10 Dokument
Logotype_04/02.eps	348 KB	Adobe Illustrator 10 Dokument
Logotype_04/03.eps	524 KB	Adobe Illustrator 10 Dokument
Logotype_04/04.eps	292 KB	Adobe Illustrator 10 Dokument
Logotype_05/01.eps	492 KB	Adobe Illustrator 10 Dokument
Skizzen	30,3 MB	Ordner
1.SchulterBlick	19,8 MB	Ordner
AA017009.JPG	60 KB	PictureViewer Dokument
AA017042.JPG	52 KB	PictureViewer Dokument
AugeRaster	120 KB	QuarkXPress Passport™ Dokument
Auge_1.tif	348 KB	Adobe Photoshop 6.0.1 Dokument
Auge_2.tif	348 KB	Adobe Photoshop 6.0.1 Dokument
Auge_3.tif	348 KB	Adobe Photoshop 6.0.1 Dokument
Auge_Kreuz.tif	348 KB	Adobe Photoshop 6.0.1 Dokument
K-Faktor	232 KB	Adobe Illustrator 10 Dokument
K-Faktor A3_1	328 KB	Adobe Illustrator 10 Dokument
K-Faktor A3_2	328 KB	Adobe Illustrator 10 Dokument
K-Faktor_2	252 KB	Adobe Illustrator 10 Dokument
K-Faktor_3	260 KB	Adobe Illustrator 10 Dokument
K-Faktor_4	140 KB	Adobe Illustrator 10 Dokument
Kirch/tf_10	88 KB	Adobe Illustrator 10 Dokument
Kirch/tf_11	84 KB	Adobe Illustrator 10 Dokument
Kirch/tf_12	92 KB	Adobe Illustrator 10 Dokument
Kirch/tf_12.1	84 KB	Adobe Illustrator 10 Dokument
Kirch/tf_12.2	84 KB	Adobe Illustrator 10 Dokument
Kirch/tf_13	92 KB	Adobe Illustrator 10 Dokument
Kirch/tf_14	92 KB	Adobe Illustrator 10 Dokument
Kirch/tf_15	92 KB	Adobe Illustrator 10 Dokument
Kirch/tf_16	92 KB	Adobe Illustrator 10 Dokument
Kirch/tf_17	84 KB	Adobe Illustrator 10 Dokument
Kirch/tf_17.1	84 KB	Adobe Illustrator 10 Dokument
Kirch/tf_17.2	88 KB	Adobe Illustrator 10 Dokument
Kirch/tf_17.3	88 KB	Adobe Illustrator 10 Dokument
Kirch/tf_17.4	88 KB	Adobe Illustrator 10 Dokument
Kirch/tf_18	88 KB	Adobe Illustrator 10 Dokument
Kirch/tf_19	88 KB	Adobe Illustrator 10 Dokument
Kirch/tf_2	84 KB	Adobe Illustrator 10 Dokument
Kirch/tf_2.1	84 KB	Adobe Illustrator 10 Dokument
Kirch/tf_2.2	84 KB	Adobe Illustrator 10 Dokument
Kirch/tf_2.3	84 KB	Adobe Illustrator 10 Dokument
Kirch/tf_2.4	84 KB	Adobe Illustrator 10 Dokument
Kirch/tf_2.5	88 KB	Adobe Illustrator 10 Dokument
Kirch/tf_2.6	84 KB	Adobe Illustrator 10 Dokument
Kirch/tf_2.7	84 KB	Adobe Illustrator 10 Dokument
Kirch/tf_20	84 KB	Adobe Illustrator 10 Dokument
Kirch/tf_20.1	88 KB	Adobe Illustrator 10 Dokument
Kirch/tf_20.2	88 KB	Adobe Illustrator 10 Dokument
Kirch/tf_21	84 KB	Adobe Illustrator 10 Dokument
Kirch/tf_21.1	88 KB	Adobe Illustrator 10 Dokument
Kirch/tf_21.1.2	88 KB	Adobe Illustrator 10 Dokument
Kirch/tf_21.2	88 KB	Adobe Illustrator 10 Dokument
Kirch/tf_21.3	88 KB	Adobe Illustrator 10 Dokument
Kirch/tf_21.4	88 KB	Adobe Illustrator 10 Dokument
Kirch/tf_21.5	92 KB	Adobe Illustrator 10 Dokument
Kirch/tf_21.6	92 KB	Adobe Illustrator 10 Dokument
Kirch/tf_22	84 KB	Adobe Illustrator 10 Dokument
Kirch/tf_22.1	88 KB	Adobe Illustrator 10 Dokument
Kirch/tf_23	84 KB	Adobe Illustrator 10 Dokument
Kirch/tf_24	84 KB	Adobe Illustrator 10 Dokument
Kirch/tf_25	84 KB	Adobe Illustrator 10 Dokument
Kirch/tf_26	84 KB	Adobe Illustrator 10 Dokument
Kirch/tf_27	84 KB	Adobe Illustrator 10 Dokument
Kirch/tf_27.1	84 KB	Adobe Illustrator 10 Dokument
Kirch/tf_28	88 KB	Adobe Illustrator 10 Dokument
Kirch/tf_28.1	88 KB	Adobe Illustrator 10 Dokument
Kirch/tf_28.2	88 KB	Adobe Illustrator 10 Dokument
Kirch/tf_28.3	88 KB	Adobe Illustrator 10 Dokument
Kirch/tf_28.4	88 KB	Adobe Illustrator 10 Dokument
Kirch/tf_29	84 KB	Adobe Illustrator 10 Dokument
Kirch/tf_29.1	84 KB	Adobe Illustrator 10 Dokument
Kirch/tf_29.2	84 KB	Adobe Illustrator 10 Dokument
Kirch/tf_29.3	84 KB	Adobe Illustrator 10 Dokument

Name	Size	Kind
Kirch/tf_3	96 KB	Adobe Illustrator
Kirch/tf_30	88 KB	Adobe Illustrator
Kirch/tf_31	88 KB	Adobe Illustrator
Kirch/tf_31.0.1	88 KB	Adobe Illustrator
Kirch/tf_31.1	88 KB	Adobe Illustrator
Kirch/tf_31.1.1	88 KB	Adobe Illustrator
Kirch/tf_31.2	88 KB	Adobe Illustrator
Kirch/tf_31.3	88 KB	Adobe Illustrator
Kirch/tf_31.3.1	88 KB	Adobe Illustrator
Kirch/tf_31.3.2	88 KB	Adobe Illustrator
Kirch/tf_31.3.3	124 KB	Adobe Illustrator
Kirch/tf_31.3.4	84 KB	Adobe Illustrator
Kirch/tf_31.3.4/0	84 KB	Adobe Illustrator
Kirch/tf_31.3.5	84 KB	Adobe Illustrator
Kirch/tf_31.3.6	80 KB	Adobe Illustrator
Kirch/tf_31.4	92 KB	Adobe Illustrator
Kirch/tf_31.4.1	92 KB	Adobe Illustrator
Kirch/tf_31.4.2	88 KB	Adobe Illustrator
Kirch/tf_31.4.3	92 KB	Adobe Illustrator
Kirch/tf_31.4.4	88 KB	Adobe Illustrator
Kirch/tf_31.4.5	88 KB	Adobe Illustrator
Kirch/tf_31.4.6	92 KB	Adobe Illustrator
Kirch/tf_31.4.7	88 KB	Adobe Illustrator
Kirch/tf_31.4.8	92 KB	Adobe Illustrator
Kirch/tf_31.5	88 KB	Adobe Illustrator
Kirch/tf_32	80 KB	Adobe Illustrator
Kirch/tf_32.1	88 KB	Adobe Illustrator
Kirch/tf_33	88 KB	Adobe Illustrator
Kirch/tf_34	88 KB	Adobe Illustrator
Kirch/tf_34.1	88 KB	Adobe Illustrator
Kirch/tf_34.2	88 KB	Adobe Illustrator
Kirch/tf_34.3	88 KB	Adobe Illustrator
Kirch/tf_35	84 KB	Adobe Illustrator
Kirch/tf_36	88 KB	Adobe Illustrator
Kirch/tf_37	88 KB	Adobe Illustrator
Kirch/tf_37.1	88 KB	Adobe Illustrator
Kirch/tf_37.2	80 KB	Adobe Illustrator
Kirch/tf_37.2.1	86 KB	Adobe Illustrator
Kirch/tf_37.3	88 KB	Adobe Illustrator
Kirch/tf_37.4	84 KB	Adobe Illustrator
Kirch/tf_38	88 KB	Adobe Illustrator
Kirch/tf_38.1	88 KB	Adobe Illustrator
Kirch/tf_38.2	88 KB	Adobe Illustrator
Kirch/tf_38.3	84 KB	Adobe Illustrator
Kirch/tf_38.32	88 KB	Adobe Illustrator
Kirch/tf_38.4	88 KB	Adobe Illustrator
Kirch/tf_39	88 KB	Adobe Illustrator
Kirch/tf_39.1	88 KB	Adobe Illustrator
Kirch/tf_39.2	88 KB	Adobe Illustrator
Kirch/tf_39.3	88 KB	Adobe Illustrator
Kirch/tf_39.4	88 KB	Adobe Illustrator
Kirch/tf_39.5	88 KB	Adobe Illustrator
Kirch/tf_39.5.1	88 KB	Adobe Illustrator
Kirch/tf_39.5.2	92 KB	Adobe Illustrator
Kirch/tf_39.5.3	88 KB	Adobe Illustrator
Kirch/tf_39.5.4	88 KB	Adobe Illustrator
Kirch/tf_39.6	88 KB	Adobe Illustrator
Kirch/tf_39.6.1	84 KB	Adobe Illustrator
Kirch/tf_39.7	88 KB	Adobe Illustrator
Kirch/tf_39.8	88 KB	Adobe Illustrator
Kirch/tf_39.9	84 KB	Adobe Illustrator
Kirch/tf_4	96 KB	Adobe Illustrator
Kirch/tf_40	84 KB	Adobe Illustrator
Kirch/tf_40.1	84 KB	Adobe Illustrator
Kirch/tf_40.2	84 KB	Adobe Illustrator
Kirch/tf_40.3	84 KB	Adobe Illustrator
Kirch/tf_41	88 KB	Adobe Illustrator
Kirch/tf_43	84 KB	Adobe Illustrator
Kirch/tf_43.1	84 KB	Adobe Illustrator
Kirch/tf_43.2	84 KB	Adobe Illustrator
Kirch/tf_43.3	84 KB	Adobe Illustrator
Kirch/tf_44	88 KB	Adobe Illustrator
Kirch/tf_44.1	88 KB	Adobe Illustrator
Kirch/tf_44.2	84 KB	Adobe Illustrator
Kirch/tf_44.3	88 KB	Adobe Illustrator
Kirch/tf_44.4	88 KB	Adobe Illustrator
Kirch/tf_45	88 KB	Adobe Illustrator
Kirch/tf_46	88 KB	Adobe Illustrator
Kirch/tf_46.0	88 KB	Adobe Illustrator
Kirch/tf_46.00	88 KB	Adobe Illustrator
Kirch/tf_46.01	88 KB	Adobe Illustrator
Kirch/tf_46.02	88 KB	Adobe Illustrator
Kirch/tf_46.03	88 KB	Adobe Illustrator
Kirch/tf_46.1	88 KB	Adobe Illustrator
Kirch/tf_46.2	88 KB	Adobe Illustrator
Kirch/tf_46.3	96 KB	Adobe Illustrator
Kirch/tf_46.4	96 KB	Adobe Illustrator
Kirch/tf_46.5	108 KB	Adobe Illustrator
Kirch/tf_46.6	88 KB	Adobe Illustrator
Kirch/tf_46.6farb	92 KB	Adobe Illustrator
Kirch/tf_46.7	96 KB	Adobe Illustrator
Kirch/tf_46.8	92 KB	Adobe Illustrator
Kirch/tf_47	88 KB	Adobe Illustrator
Kirch/tf_47.1	88 KB	Adobe Illustrator
Kirch/tf_47.2	88 KB	Adobe Illustrator
Kirch/tf_47.3	104 KB	Adobe Illustrator
Kirch/tf_48	88 KB	Adobe Illustrator
Kirch/tf_49	88 KB	Adobe Illustrator
Kirch/tf_5	92 KB	Adobe Illustrator
Kirch/tf_50	88 KB	Adobe Illustrator
Kirch/tf_50.1	88 KB	Adobe Illustrator
Kirch/tf_50.2	88 KB	Adobe Illustrator
Kirch/tf_50.3	88 KB	Adobe Illustrator
Kirch/tf_51	88 KB	Adobe Illustrator
Kirch/tf_51.1	88 KB	Adobe Illustrator
Kirch/tf_51.1.1	80 KB	Adobe Illustrator
Kirch/tf_51.1a	92 KB	Adobe Illustrator
Kirch/tf_51.1b	88 KB	Adobe Illustrator
Kirch/tf_51.1c	88 KB	Adobe Illustrator
Kirch/tf_51.1d	88 KB	Adobe Illustrator
Kirch/tf_51.1e	88 KB	Adobe Illustrator
Kirch/tf_51.2	88 KB	Adobe Illustrator
Kirch/tf_51.2a	88 KB	Adobe Illustrator
Kirch/tf_51.2b	88 KB	Adobe Illustrator
Kirch/tf_51.2c	88 KB	Adobe Illustrator
Kirch/tf_52	88 KB	Adobe Illustrator
Kirch/tf_53	136 KB	Adobe Illustrator
Kirch/tf_53.1	136 KB	Adobe Illustrator
Kirch/tf_54	88 KB	Adobe Illustrator
Kirch/tf_56	80 KB	Adobe Illustrator
Kirch/tf_57	88 KB	Adobe Illustrator
Kirch/tf_58	88 KB	Adobe Illustrator
Kirch/tf_59	84 KB	Adobe Illustrator
Kirch/tf_6	88 KB	Adobe Illustrator
Kirch/tf_6.1	88 KB	Adobe Illustrator
Kirch/tf_6.2	84 KB	Adobe Illustrator
Kirch/tf_6.3	88 KB	Adobe Illustrator
Kirch/tf_6.3.0	88 KB	Adobe Illustrator
Kirch/tf_6.4	88 KB	Adobe Illustrator
Kirch/tf_60	88 KB	Adobe Illustrator

Name	Size	Kind
Kirch/tf_62	88 KB	Adobe Illustrator 10 Dokument
Kirch/tf_7	84 KB	Adobe Illustrator 10 Dokument
Kirch/tf_8	84 KB	Adobe Illustrator 10 Dokument
Kirch/tf_9	84 KB	Adobe Illustrator 10 Dokument
Kombination_1	100 KB	Adobe Illustrator 10 Dokument
Kombination_2	108 KB	Adobe Illustrator 10 Dokument
Kombination_3	112 KB	Adobe Illustrator 10 Dokument
2.welle	6,4 MB	Ordner
#1Kirch_1	84 KB	Adobe Illustrator 10 Dokument
#1Kirch_2	84 KB	Adobe Illustrator 10 Dokument
Auge_tf	2,3 MB	Ordner
Kirch/Auge_1.0	84 KB	Adobe Illustrator 10 Dokument
Kirch/Auge_1.1	84 KB	Adobe Illustrator 10 Dokument
Kirch/Auge_1.2	84 KB	Adobe Illustrator 10 Dokument
Kirch/Auge_1.3	84 KB	Adobe Illustrator 10 Dokument
Kirch/Auge_2	84 KB	Adobe Illustrator 10 Dokument
Kirch/Auge_2.0	84 KB	Adobe Illustrator 10 Dokument
Kirch/Auge_2.1	84 KB	Adobe Illustrator 10 Dokument
Kirch/Auge_3.0	84 KB	Adobe Illustrator 10 Dokument
Kirch/Auge_3.1	84 KB	Adobe Illustrator 10 Dokument
Kirch/Auge_3.10	88 KB	Adobe Illustrator 10 Dokument
Kirch/Auge_3.11	88 KB	Adobe Illustrator 10 Dokument
Kirch/Auge_3.2	84 KB	Adobe Illustrator 10 Dokument
Kirch/Auge_3.3	184 KB	Adobe Illustrator 10 Dokument
Kirch/Auge_3.4	84 KB	Adobe Illustrator 10 Dokument
Kirch/Auge_3.5	84 KB	Adobe Illustrator 10 Dokument
Kirch/Auge_3.6	84 KB	Adobe Illustrator 10 Dokument
Kirch/Auge_3.7	84 KB	Adobe Illustrator 10 Dokument
Kirch/Auge_3.8	84 KB	Adobe Illustrator 10 Dokument
Kirch/Auge_3.9	84 KB	Adobe Illustrator 10 Dokument
Kirch/Auge_4.0	84 KB	Adobe Illustrator 10 Dokument
Kirch/Auge_4.1	84 KB	Adobe Illustrator 10 Dokument
Kirch/Auge_4.2	84 KB	Adobe Illustrator 10 Dokument
Kirch/Auge_4.3	88 KB	Adobe Illustrator 10 Dokument
Kirch/Auge_5.0	84 KB	Adobe Illustrator 10 Dokument
Kirch/Auge_5.1	84 KB	Adobe Illustrator 10 Dokument
Kirch/Auge_5.2	88 KB	Adobe Illustrator 10 Dokument
Kirch/Auge_5.3	86 KB	Adobe Illustrator 10 Dokument
AxelAuge_1	84 KB	Adobe Illustrator 10 Dokument
Kirch/Auge_3.5	84 KB	Adobe Illustrator 10 Dokument
Kirch/Auge_3.6	84 KB	Adobe Illustrator 10 Dokument
Kirch/klammer_1.1	84 KB	Adobe Illustrator 10 Dokument
Kirch/tf_62	96 KB	Adobe Illustrator 10 Dokument
Kirch/tf_65	92 KB	Adobe Illustrator 10 Dokument
Kirch/tf_65.0	84 KB	Adobe Illustrator 10 Dokument
Kirch/tf_65.01	84 KB	Adobe Illustrator 10 Dokument
Kirch/tf_65.02	84 KB	Adobe Illustrator 10 Dokument
Kirch/tf_65.03	84 KB	Adobe Illustrator 10 Dokument
Kirch/tf_65.04	84 KB	Adobe Illustrator 10 Dokument
Kirch/tf_65.05	84 KB	Adobe Illustrator 10 Dokument
Kirch/tf_65.06	84 KB	Adobe Illustrator 10 Dokument
Kirch/tf_65.07	84 KB	Adobe Illustrator 10 Dokument
Kirch/tf_65.07farbig	92 KB	Adobe Illustrator 10 Dokument
Kirch/tf_65.07farbig2	92 KB	Adobe Illustrator 10 Dokument
Kirch/tf_65.08	84 KB	Adobe Illustrator 10 Dokument
Kirch/tf_65.0farbig	84 KB	Adobe Illustrator 10 Dokument
Kirch/tf_65.02	84 KB	Adobe Illustrator 10 Dokument
Kirch/tf_65.03	84 KB	Adobe Illustrator 10 Dokument
Kirch/tf_65.04	84 KB	Adobe Illustrator 10 Dokument
Kirch/tf_65.05	84 KB	Adobe Illustrator 10 Dokument
Kirch/tf_65.06	84 KB	Adobe Illustrator 10 Dokument
Kirch/tf_65.07	84 KB	Adobe Illustrator 10 Dokument
Kirch/tf_65.07farbig	92 KB	Adobe Illustrator 10 Dokument
Kirch/tf_65.07farbig2	92 KB	Adobe Illustrator 10 Dokument
Kirch/tf_65.08	84 KB	Adobe Illustrator 10 Dokument
Kirch/tf_65.0farbig	84 KB	Adobe Illustrator 10 Dokument
Kirch/tf_65.1	96 KB	Adobe Illustrator 10 Dokument
Kirch/tf_65.2	84 KB	Adobe Illustrator 10 Dokument
Kirch/tf_65.3	84 KB	Adobe Illustrator 10 Dokument
Kirch/tf_65.4	84 KB	Adobe Illustrator 10 Dokument
Kirch/tf_66	96 KB	Adobe Illustrator 10 Dokument
Kirch/tf_67	96 KB	Adobe Illustrator 10 Dokument
Kirch/tf_67.1	96 KB	Adobe Illustrator 10 Dokument
Kirch/tf_67.2	96 KB	Adobe Illustrator 10 Dokument
Kirch/tf_68	96 KB	Adobe Illustrator 10 Dokument
Kirch/tf_69	92 KB	Adobe Illustrator 10 Dokument
Kirch/tf_69.1	92 KB	Adobe Illustrator 10 Dokument
Kirch/tf_70.0	92 KB	Adobe Illustrator 10 Dokument
Kirch/tf_71	84 KB	Adobe Illustrator 10 Dokument
Kirch/tf_71.0	96 KB	Adobe Illustrator 10 Dokument
Kirch/tf_71.1	84 KB	Adobe Illustrator 10 Dokument
Kirch/tf_71.2	88 KB	Adobe Illustrator 10 Dokument
Kirch/tf_71.3	88 KB	Adobe Illustrator 10 Dokument
Kirch/tf_71.4	84 KB	Adobe Illustrator 10 Dokument
Kirch/tf_72	84 KB	Adobe Illustrator 10 Dokument
Kirch/tf_72.0	96 KB	Adobe Illustrator 10 Dokument
Kirch/tf_74	84 KB	Adobe Illustrator 10 Dokument
Kirch/tf_75	84 KB	Adobe Illustrator 10 Dokument
Klemme	84 KB	Ordner
Kirch/klammer_1.0	84 KB	Adobe Illustrator 10 Dokument
Logo/Systematik	92 KB	Adobe Illustrator 10 Dokument
Logo/Systematik_0.1	96 KB	Adobe Illustrator 10 Dokument
Logo/Systematik_1	92 KB	Adobe Illustrator 10 Dokument
Logo/Systematik_1.1	96 KB	Adobe Illustrator 10 Dokument
Logo/Systematik_2	92 KB	Adobe Illustrator 10 Dokument
Fuzz Kreis.psd	232 KB	Adobe® Photoshop® 6.0.1 Dokument
Fuzz Kreis.tif	1,9 MB	Adobe® Photoshop® 6.0.1 Dokument
Fuzz Kreis_2.psd	208 KB	Adobe® Photoshop® 6.0.1 Dokument
FuzzEck.tif	844 KB	Adobe® Photoshop® 6.0.1 Dokument
Fuzz/Fuzz Kreis.tif	844 KB	Adobe® Photoshop® 6.0.1 Dokument

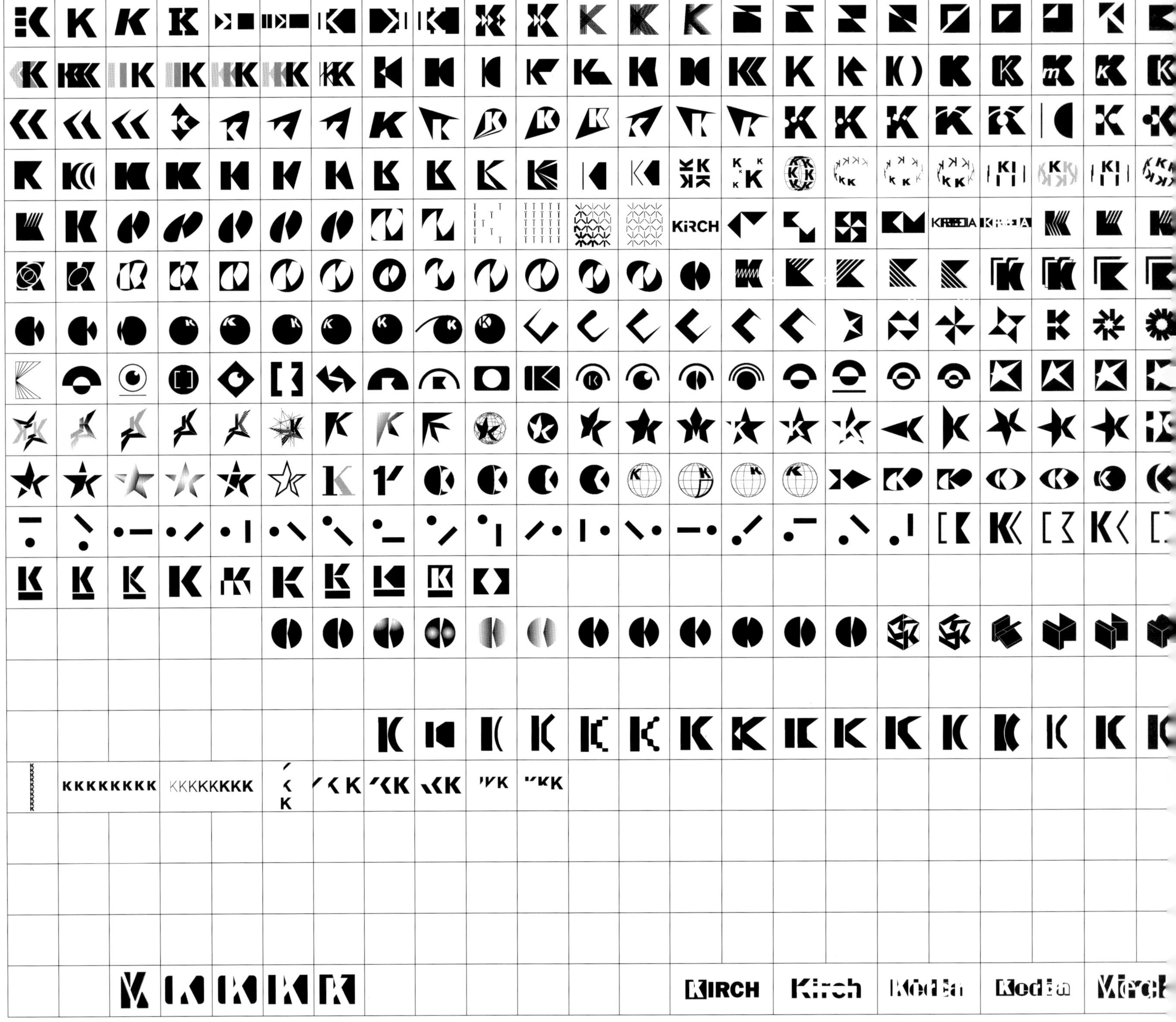
KIRCH
KMEDIA
KIRCH
Kirch
Media
Media
Kirch

Client KirchMedia, Munich
Project Corporate design

Brief Following the planned merger of KirchMedia with ProSiebenSat.1, a new positioning of the resulting company was required, even though the KirchMedia name would remain.
The new logo or symbol to be developed should clearly place KirchMedia in the centre of the fully integrated media partnership, and convey the full profile of the new enterprise.

Concept Because of the long-running corporate narrative behind Kirch, it was decided to maintain the letter K as the kernel element in the new logo. It was derived from moving images, not from static graphics and so appropriate for a moving medium.
The new symbol is the base element in the complete overlay, a visual analogy to the structure of the vertically integrated media group. The letter 'K' is clearly in the foreground, linked to the header letter of the various sub-brands (Media, Sport and Entertainment.) To achieve this a typographical system based on a square was developed: this allowed the mark to work in moving media, for example as a trailer or animation. This system sets the way for both the holding company and subsidiaries to develop a co-ordinated identity system for themselves and their affiliates. It would use colour coding and type changes to establish the necessary hierarchies. The new mark was intended to have a central position in the corporate communication structure, both on-screen and in photographs.

Comment the financial difficulties of the client meant that this project was stopped at the key concept level. But it was already clear by then that the new concept had the potential to convey accurately the identity of the client.

KIRCHmedia
KIRCHsport
KIRCHentertainment

"For a moment of lightning
   your eyes recover
   their innocence:
   the sky
   is drawn on a background of trees,
   the message for you is white."
Günter Eich, Lesson from a Storm

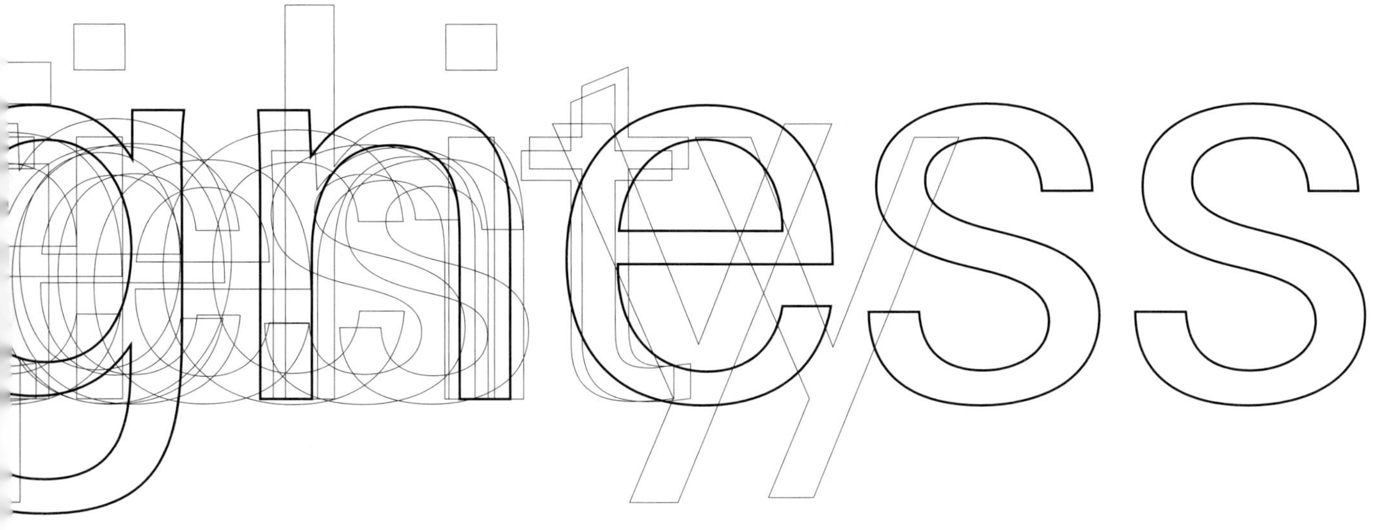

Nothingness The old Aristotelian principle that Nature abhors a vacuum blinded people for a long time to the elegance of emptiness, to the spaces between the columns that make the grace of the façade, or the white around and within the letters that is the key to legibility and charm. Today science tells us differently: even the black deeps of space are full of dark matter. The opposite of presence is not nothing, but a different kind of presence.

A design can also seem to contain nothingness in the way that it handles the empty space: between the text and the page edges, between the piazza and the street, between the music and the words. But this absence is not nothingness: it has to be set in the same language, follow the same diction, as the rest of the design.

But nothingness—the no thing—is also the starting point of design: tabula rasa is where it begins. With no preconceptions. Starting off thinking that one is going to design something can put up barriers to being creative. But once the decision is taken about what should be designed, then a whole range of ideas and concepts about how design should be done may come into play.

Yet often even in the finished result the designer's intervention may appear minimal, even abstract, like the presence of a director in a film: behind the camera and so beyond the screen. This is not minimalism as a design solution, rather a principle of reduction that does not seek to intervene beyond a necessary level. Often this may be because the designer has simply acted as a conduit, bringing out of the client what the client already knew but could not formulate. And even if the designer does add to what the client knows, this addition is only succesful if there is transparency between the designer and the client. The client who arrives with preconceptions is as much a problem as the designer who has preconceived ideas about what is going to be designed. So the best design, ironically, starts from nothing, and adds nothing to create something.

Client Lamborghini, Sant'Agata Bolognese
Project Launch of the Murciélago and trade fair stand.

Brief Uncompromising, extreme, male, aggressive, dangerous: these are the keywords for Lamborghini and were the basis for KMS's approach to launching the Murciélago model at an event by Mount Etna in Sicily and at the IAA 2001 show in Frankfurt. The word Murciélago is Spanish for a bat, but the name also comes from a bull so brave it was spared by the matador Rafael Molina, nick-named Lagartijo. KMS also developed a typographic style for the name appropriate to the values of the new Lamborghini.

Concept The lettering of the Murciélago name is classical and restrained, monolithic. It rises from its base edge, to make a single sculptural relief form. This powerful and dramatic effect was what was sought in the launch and the stand. The launch took place in the shadow of Mount Etna, or rather in the light of an eruption, the force of nature an emblematic echo of the power of the brand. The car drove past at speed, was glimpsed for a moment and vanished, bat-like, immediately in the dark. Black night and yellow lava: even Nature seemed to wear Lamborghini colours.
The fair stand was a structured, almost sacral event. On a black stand, three black boxes. Each rose to reveal two cars and the engine unit. Inside the lifted boxes, the hollow shape where the car had nestled, lost but matching forms. A symbolic birth in steel, combining elegance and power.

Comment At the heart of the brand personality of Lamborghini lies what might be termed an automobile myth, which flows through and into their products. KMS had to use the presence—or absence—of the cars to convey that mythic quality.

"How can I know what I think till I see what I say?"
Quoted by E. M. Forster

Philosophy Alan Fletcher, one of the founders of Pentagram, quotes a suggestion to divide design companies into two categories: helicopters and vending machines. The helicopter could move around a project, looking at it from different distances and angles, and devise an independent solution. With the vending machine, the clients put their money in and whatever was in the machine popped out. It's a vigorous, not to say bizarre, comparison. (One can think of plenty of agencies which the vending machine concept fits perfectly, sad to say.) Helicopters are a good metaphor, as they are in a way counterintuitive machines – they can hover, they even fly backwards. They operate by a unique set of rules. They have ambiguity, being both warcraft and rescue vehicles. Each mission is different, unlike life for the vending machine. With a vending machine you know what you are getting. For a Pacific islander speaking pidgin English a helicopter is 'Mixmaster him belong Jesus Christ,' a poetic and ironic description that neatly conflates missionary zeal and consumer goodies. (Though as helicopters are more common in the Pacific than kitchen appliances, it may be that pidgin English for a Mixmaster should be 'helicopter him belong kitchen.')

Many design companies profess a design philosophy. If that means they are motivated by broader ideas than turnover or profit, that's a step in the right direction. If that means they have policies about opportunity, equality and responsibility, that is even better. But if a design philosophy becomes a dogma, only a way of doing things, that is a step backwards. A design philosophy should be a way of looking at the world, not a metaphor for metaphysics. A design company's philosophy should be about its future, not its past. It should question the validity of how it has got where it is as a means of defining better how to move forward, how to be responsible and responsive. Not where you start from but the motor to get you where you want to be: fire up the Mixmaster, the sky's the limit, as it were.

Client Villa Stuck, Munich
Project Corporate design and communications

Brief The Villa Stuck, former home of the painter Franz von Stuck is today a famous museum, with an exhibitions programme of modern fine and applied art, especially from the Art Nouveau era. In 1993 the Villa commissioned a new identity from KMS, to reflect both its traditional role and its place in today's social and artistic discourse. The new identity has since been developed and applied to posters, invitations and publications, as well as to the building's internal and external signage.

Concept A label originally used by Franz von Stuck became the starting point for developing the new logo: a form on a square ground introduces, as a sort of architectural game, the idea of the house, while giving the whole a timeless and classic quality. For the communications design the programme of changing exhibitions provided the overall concept. Developing the logo in turn created a grid pattern as a basis for printed work, and a prominent use of typography completed the process.

Comment In nearly a decade of partnership KMS has produced over fifty posters for different exhibitions from fine arts, applied arts, architecture, industrial arts, graphic design to photography. Throughout the aim has been not to display the designer's virtuosity but rather to demonstrate the diversity of the Villa Stuck's programme.

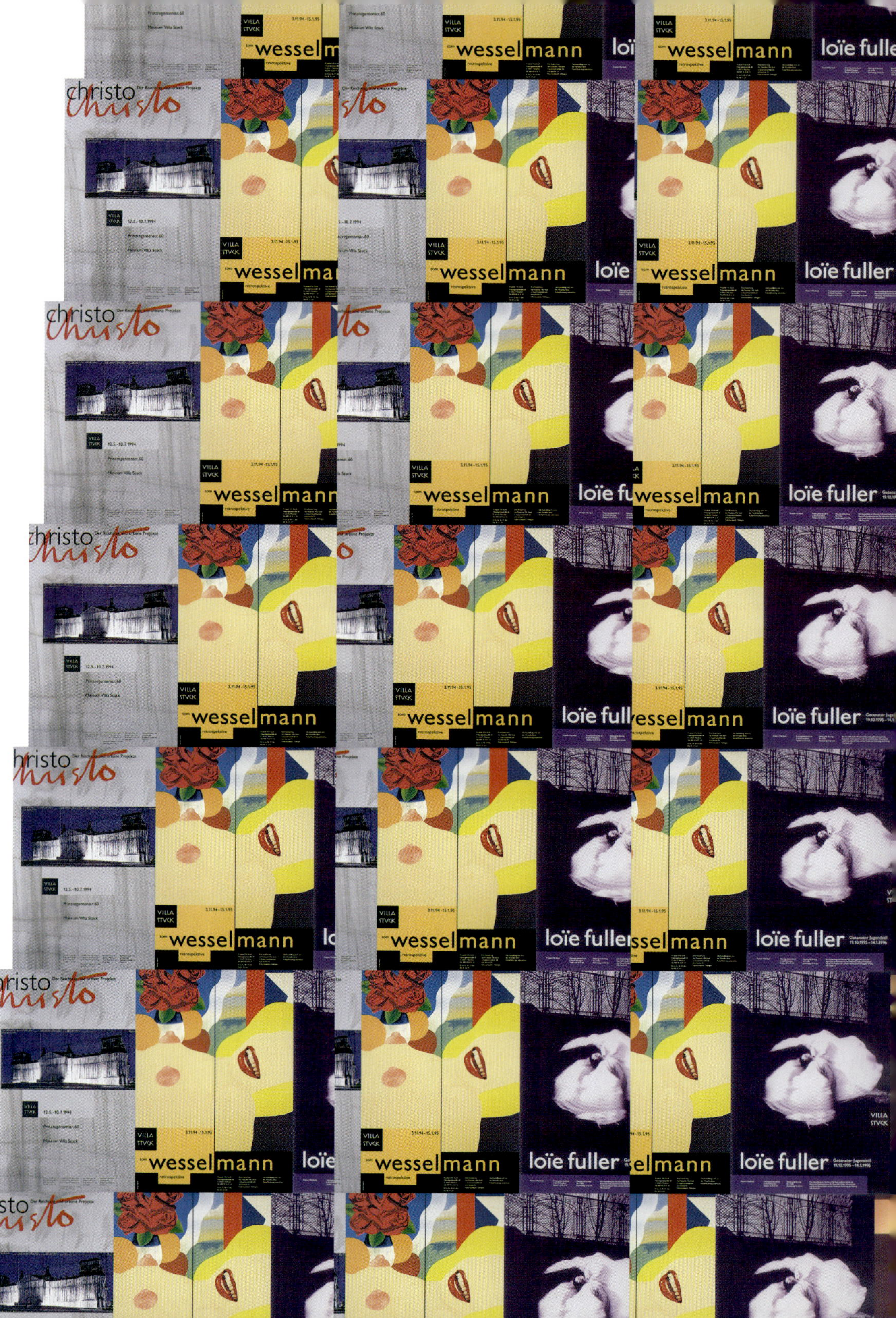

loïe fuller
Getanzter Jugendstil
15.12.1995 – 14.1.1996
VILLA STVCK
marina abramović
Installationen 8.2.– 8.4.1996
VILLA STVCK
helen levitt
VILLA STVCK
japan
VILLA STVCK
Theater

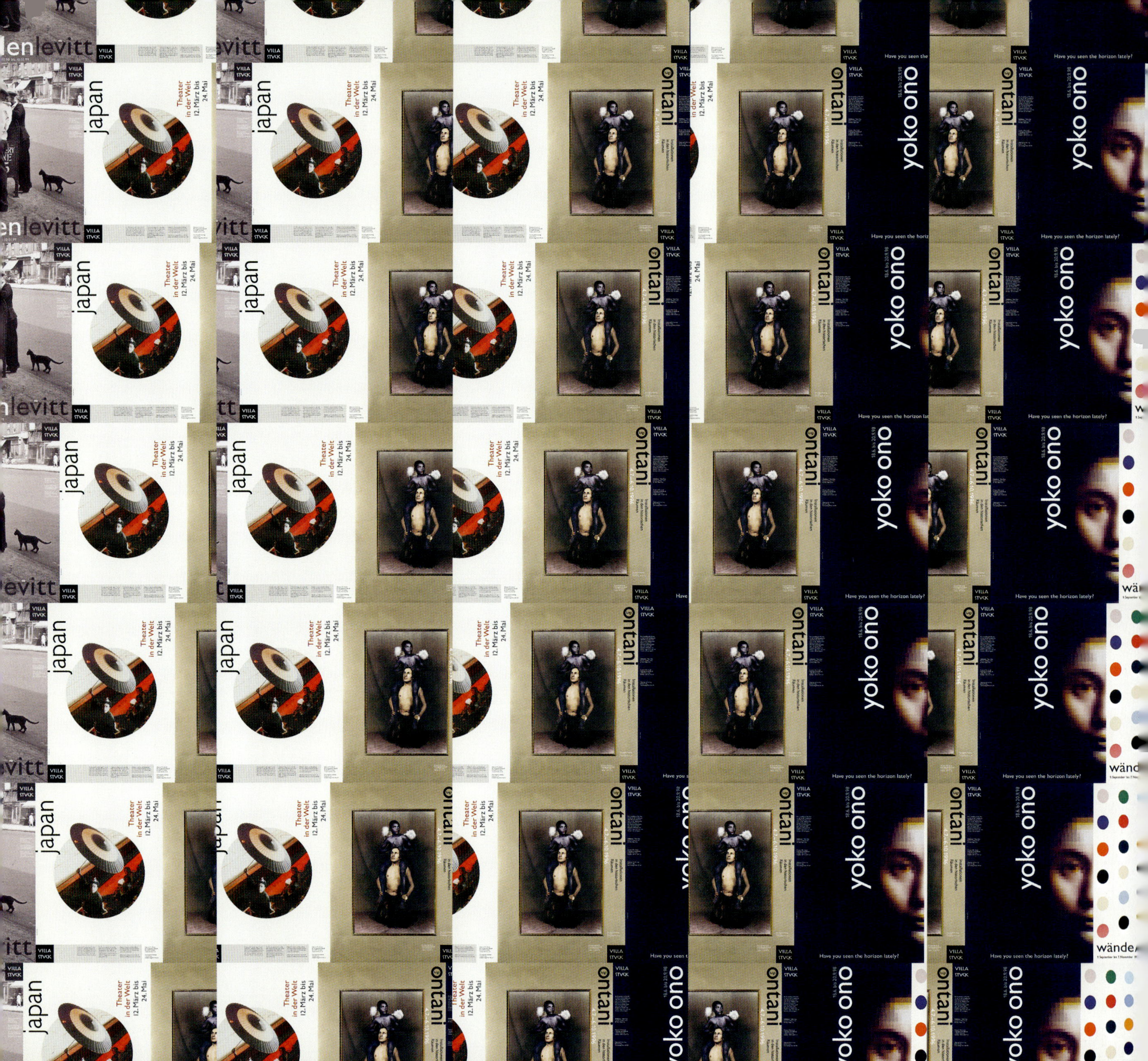

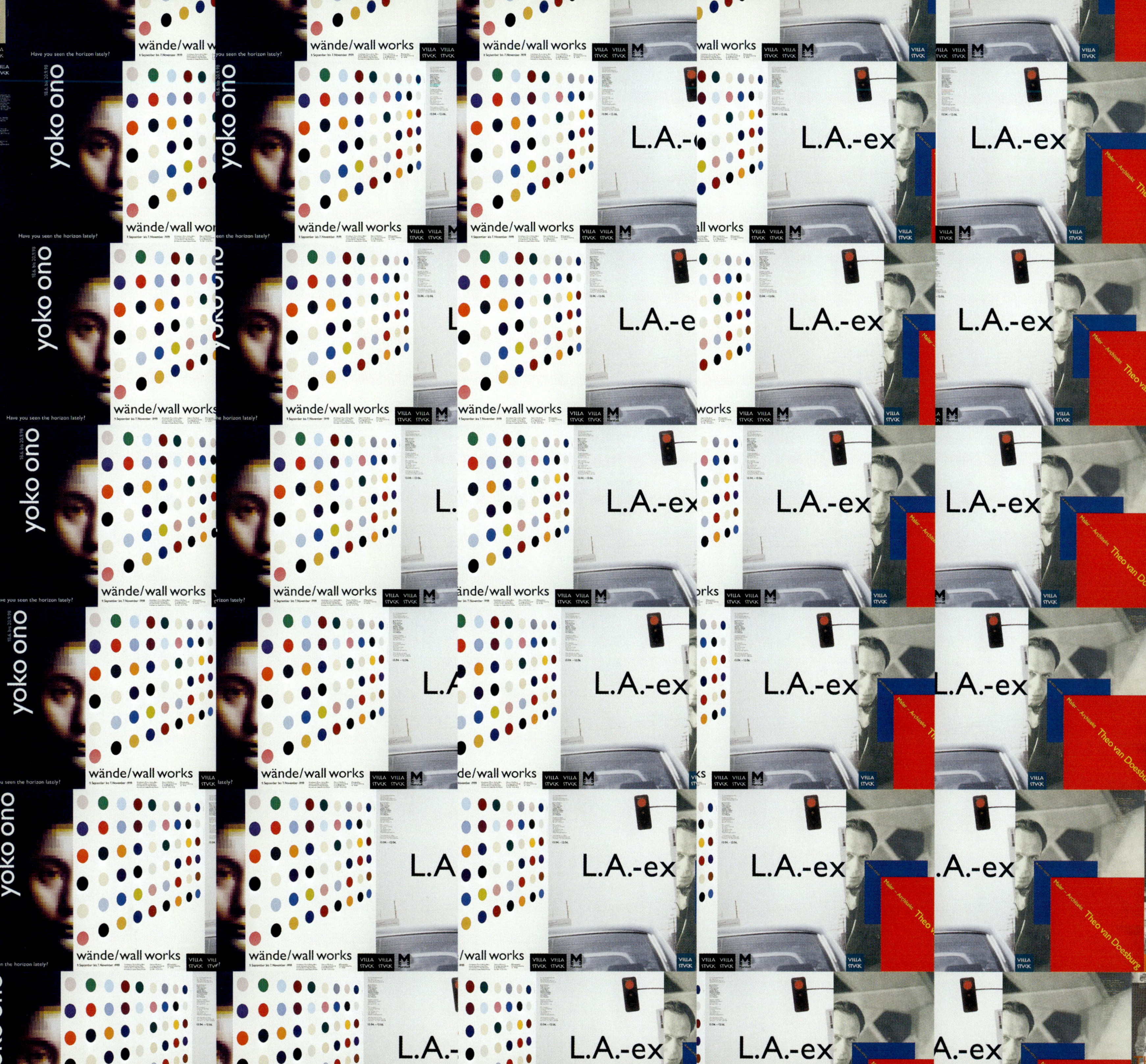

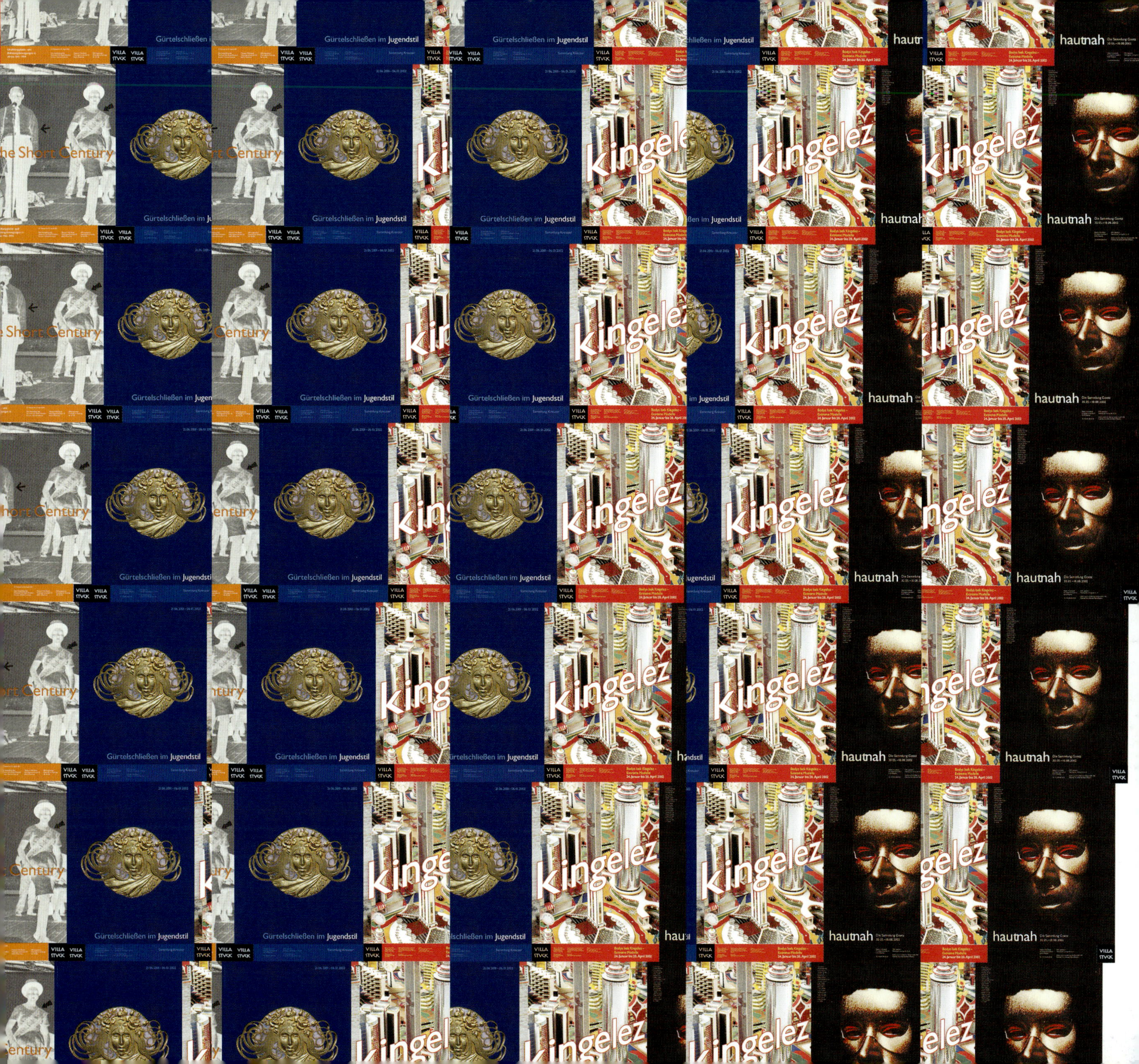

"A poem should be wordless
 As the flight of birds"
 Archibald MacLeish, Ars Poetica

Courage In 1960 the artist Jean Tinguely was offered an exhibition at the Museum of Modern Art in New York. As well as showing some of his existing pieces, enormous and pointless noisy machines welded together from scrap, he also created a new machine, entitled Homage to New York, incorporating flamethrowers and fountains, in the garden of the Museum. It was turned for the private view, to the delight of the art crowd and the consternation of the New York Fire Department, who eventually insisted on stopping the machine by smashing it. It is the Farenheit 451 moment of post-War art, redolent of symbolism. It is not certain whether the intervention of the Borough's Finest with their fire-axes was part of the original plan (though some describe the machine as 'self-destructing'), and I personally never quite believed the story of the firefighters weeping as they wielded (I rather suspect that they saw the whole thing as absolutely subversive.)

The aspect that gets overlooked is Tinguely's courage. A show at MoMA was the ultimate accolade, the absolute imprimatur. To risk all that on what might be made to work from the objets trouves in the junk-yards of Brooklyn was incredible. It was a gesture that required astonishing confidence — or astonishing folly.

Courage is not about conformity, about esprit de corps in the sense of discipline and honour: bravery might be, but bravery is more often about folly as well. Courage is about confidence and will, about having the assurance to try the option, to take the risk. Courage in design (and there are design follies as well) is not only about the solution, but about

having the initial conviction to go for it, and the perseverance to convince others — clients, partners — to follow you.
One of Tinguely's friends and mentors was the artist Yves Klein, who also made paintings with fire and air. One of his famous works was 'Le Saut dans le Vide' where he simply jumped off a balcony. Asked why, he simply replied that any created work was a leap into the void.

off
drive
off
venir c'est
zukunft ist
Zukunft Audi
(savon)
avon)
Evolution techno
e. π
Aa
Katalog
bis
A8 A6
(co
L'avei
L'ave
(sac)
aire et r
esoins c
fast forward
bar

Client Audi, Ingolstadt
Project Concept for A series international motorshow stands, 1997—2002

Concept Complete communications design for trade fair stands, including off-site events and advertising, visitor relations, invitations, vehicle presentations, event staging, stand motto and graphics, lighting, film and video, sound effects, kid's club, VIP lounges, press services, press conference and pack, gifts and promotional items.

Comment KMS's designs were first shown at the IAA Frankfurt 1997, and later at: Tokyo Motor Show 1997, 1999, 2001; Salon International de l'Automobile Genf 1997—2001; Mondial de l'Automobile Paris 1998, 2000; IAA Frankfurt 1999, 2001; NAIAS Detroit 1998—2002.

Client Mercedes-Benz, Stuttgart
Project Exhibition stand at the Mondial de l'Automobile,
Paris 2002

Brief The communication concept for the Paris motor
show has safety at its centre, safety as expressed by the
newest technological developments and by the established competence of the car-maker.

Concept The design uses a circular layout for the elements. Along the radii of the central circle, semi-transpa-
rent walls, four metres by six, divide the area into bays,
one for each model, with the central area—the compass
rose—for special presentations. The wall surfaces carry
comments and messages about safety features, as well
as information about the adjacent models. Three of the
walls also house large LED screens for showing linked
visual presentations and animations. Radial lines link
the wall bases to the central arena.

Comments The concept integrates symbolic and functional aspects of the safety concept. The circle is an Ur-
mark, the walls ramparts of protection. The radial layout
welcomes the visitor in and yet suggests protection.
The pared-down visual language implies the sovereignty
and established role of the Mercedes Benz marque.
KMS felt the concept to be a very powerful one, even
though the final design when it opens will be different.

Crash
rbag

SAFE
SBC
PRE-SAFE
Crash-Sensorik
Crash-Sen
Airbag
ABC
E-Klasse
TEST
LÄNGE

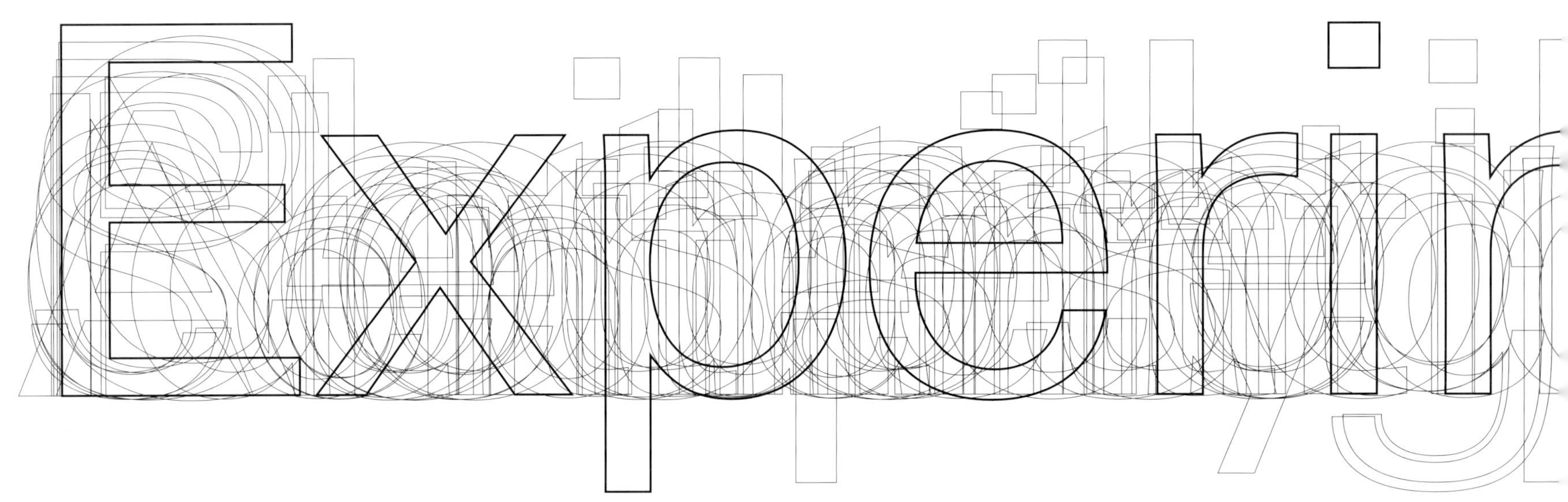

A traveller at an Irish railway station asked the guard if he could get a train from there to Cork. The guard paused a moment, then replied 'if I wanted to go there, sir, I'd not start from here…'

Experiment Take the French philosopher Baudrillard's comments on the object of consumption, and turn them, carefully, on their head. Look at them not from the point of view of what they mean for the consumer, but for what they have to say about the designer. Baudrillard tells us that the consumer is either the happy recipient of the endless bounty of invention created for his — or her — individual enjoyment, or the hapless victim of relentless capitalist pressure towards reckless acquisition. This marxist/market dichotomy leaves the designer as either the mayfly cheerleader of consumer hedonism or the slave of the market in a market of slaves. Neither makes for a very attractive figure, but then neither coincides with our vision of the designer today.

Baudrillard is, of course, right when he says that the object of consumption only exists because a language of consumption exists around it. And he is right to say that there are radically opposed political approaches to interpreting the language of consumption. Writing in the 1970s, he was entitled to remind his readers of that polarity and its dangers. Thirty years on we would be foolish to assume that the danger disappeared with the Berlin wall. But that event, if it did not end the dichotomy, did at least open other possibilities, other ways of reading the language.

Designers cannot escape their place within the nexus of consumption (whether even artists can do so is an undecided issue.) But what designers can, and perhaps must do, is extend the dialogue, develop new tools to interpret the situation. Design must experiment. Not just in the sense of enjoying new technologies and new materials, new media and new products, but experiment in the sense of making those novelties accessible to the existing framework, and so extending its power to enrich and delight the world—and make it think as well.

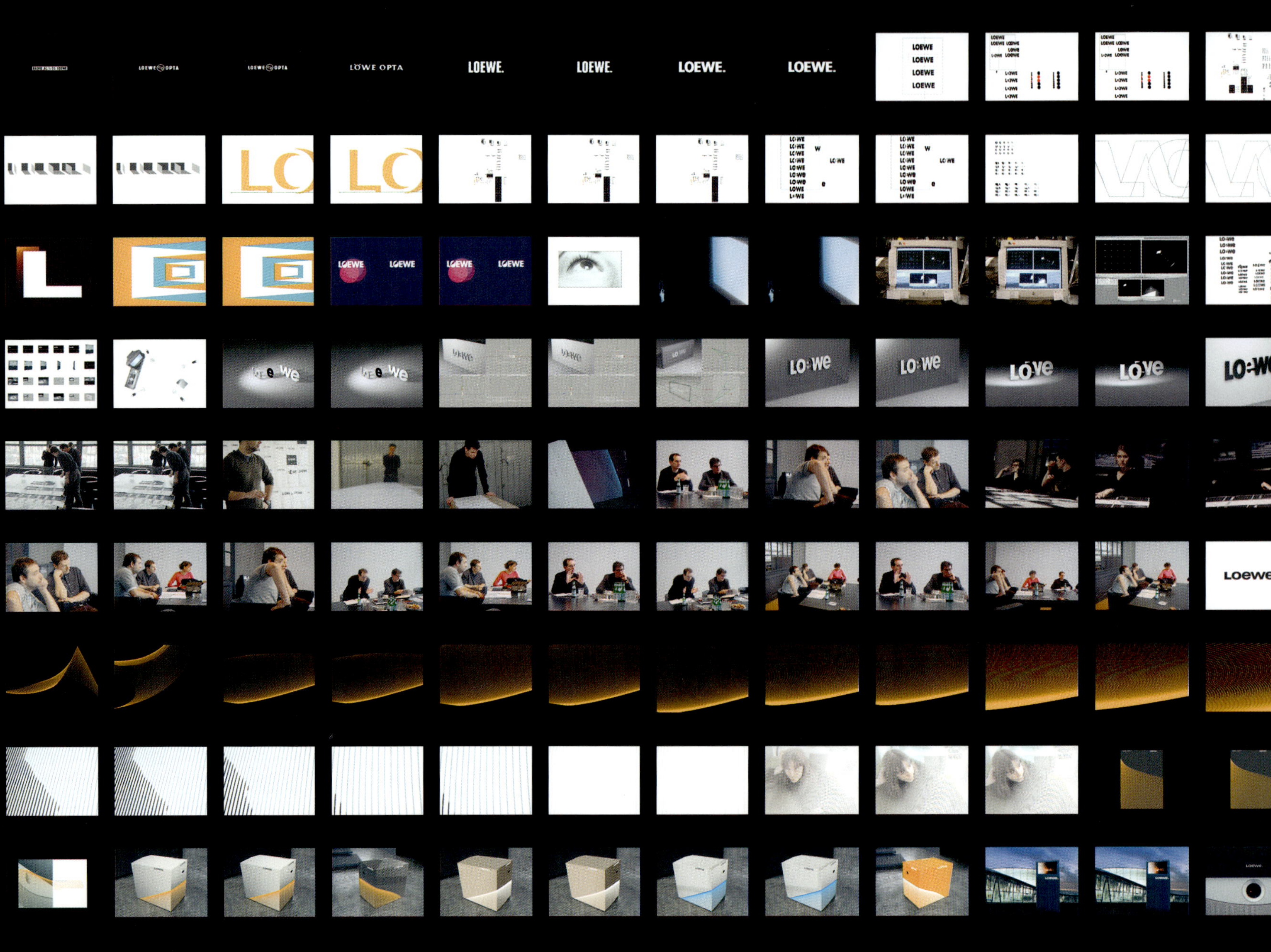

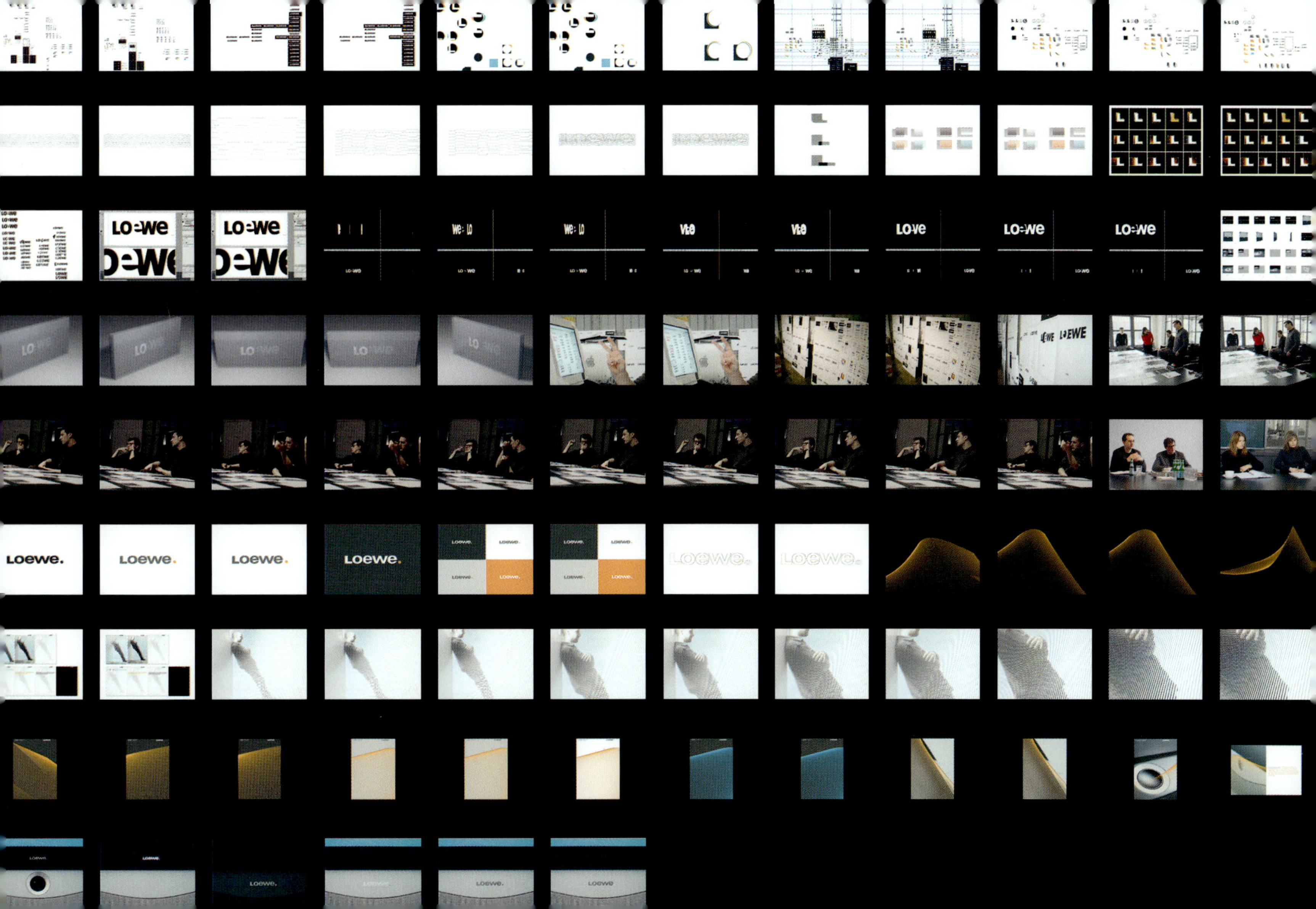

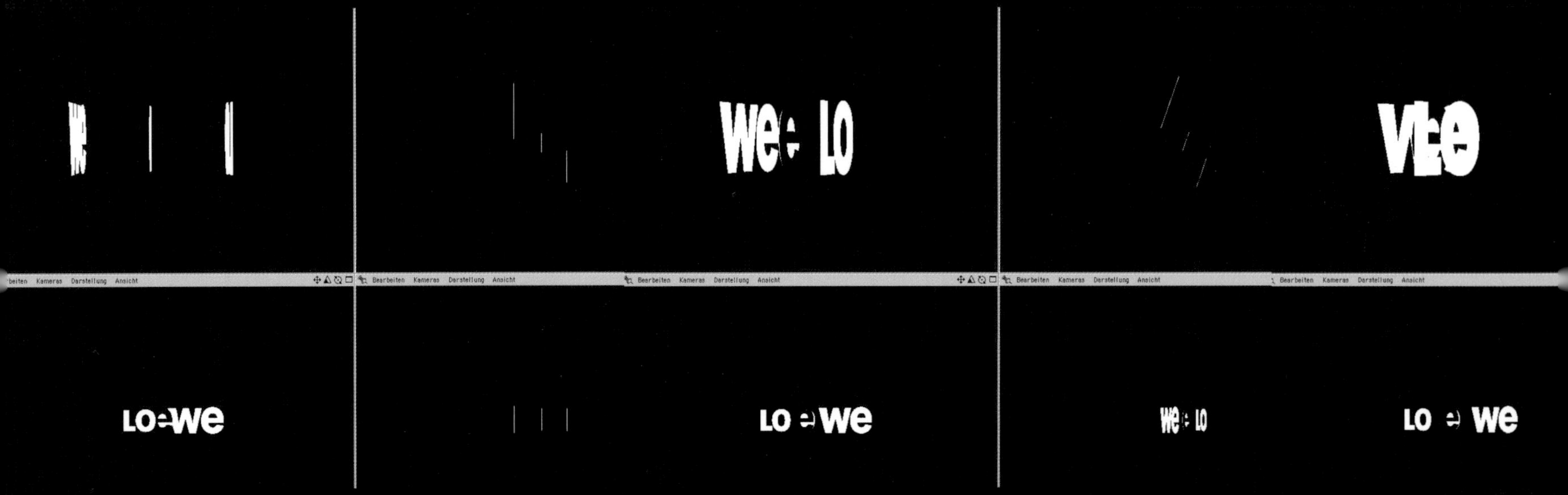
Bearbeiten Kameras Darstellung Ansicht
LO=WE

LOve
LO=we
Bearbeiten Kameras Darstellung Ansicht
Bearbeiten Kameras Darstellung Ansicht
Bearbeiten Kameras Darstellung Ansicht
Bearbeiten Kameras Darstellung Ansicht
Bn Kameras Darstellung Ansicht
LOve
LO=we

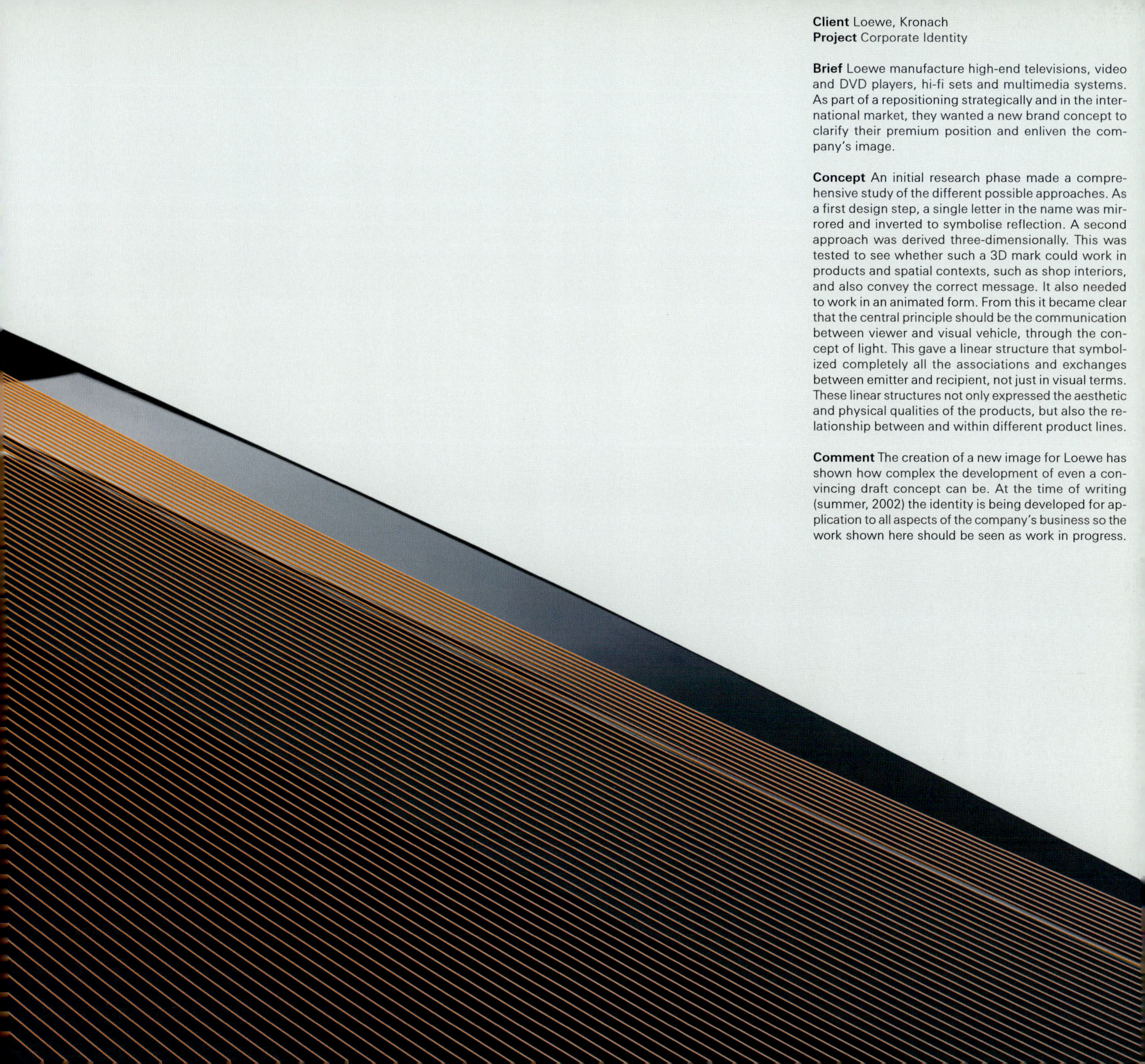

Client Loewe, Kronach
Project Corporate Identity

Brief Loewe manufacture high-end televisions, video and DVD players, hi-fi sets and multimedia systems. As part of a repositioning strategically and in the international market, they wanted a new brand concept to clarify their premium position and enliven the company's image.

Concept An initial research phase made a comprehensive study of the different possible approaches. As a first design step, a single letter in the name was mirrored and inverted to symbolise reflection. A second approach was derived three-dimensionally. This was tested to see whether such a 3D mark could work in products and spatial contexts, such as shop interiors, and also convey the correct message. It also needed to work in an animated form. From this it became clear that the central principle should be the communication between viewer and visual vehicle, through the concept of light. This gave a linear structure that symbolized completely all the associations and exchanges between emitter and recipient, not just in visual terms. These linear structures not only expressed the aesthetic and physical qualities of the products, but also the relationship between and within different product lines.

Comment The creation of a new image for Loewe has shown how complex the development of even a convincing draft concept can be. At the time of writing (summer, 2002) the identity is being developed for application to all aspects of the company's business so the work shown here should be seen as work in progress.

"Just as the blueprint of a building isn't the building itself, every science
means a schematized picture of reality."
Ludwig von Bertalanffy, General System Theory

Possibilities "Eine Wissenschaft, aber nicht Wissenschaft", as Kant described chemistry. Or rather as D'Arcy Wentworth Thompson quotes Kant in the opening pages of his magisterial work On Growth and Form. For Thompson argues that, like chemistry in the past, the biology and physiology of his day are sciences but not Science, since they had not been studied using mathematical and physical methods and principles. This he proceeded to do over nearly 800 pages, in the first edition of 1917. His work, by its very erudition and scope, annoyed many of his contemporaries, and the recognition he deserved was late and long in coming. Today we see that mathematics and physics are key tools in our understanding of the natural world, and it is hard to realise just how radical Thompson's view was eight decades ago.

D'Arcy Thompson seeks to analyse how earlier thinkers had missed this central point, that mathematics was the gateway and key to all science. Some had assumed, following Aristotle, that philosophy was the correct approach, others nature, others medicine. Many had shared, wittingly or unwittingly, a view propounded by Aristotle and supported by the Bible, that of teleological explanation. This suggests that the final form of something (an animal or a plant), its end (telos in Greek) is both the result and the cause of its earlier progression and development. Darwin's theories of 'survival of the fittest' and Huxley's gloss on them both also supported the view that the natural order was, in some way, ordered. It seems to me that histories of design, and some accounts of contemporary design, also suffer from the teleological urge. Pevsner's

Pioneers of Modern Design is a classic example, where he expunges from his history those like Sant'Elia, Gaudí and the Futurists who do not conform to his crusade for the importance of Modernism. Today, there is a general assumption that design is the way it is because of history and circumstances. While it is evident that economic and social forces have shaped the current role and position of design and designing, it does not follow that the contemporary designer is the fittest creature to perform the tasks expected of it. Or, put another way, if one was to design a designer today ab initio, perhaps the result would be very different.

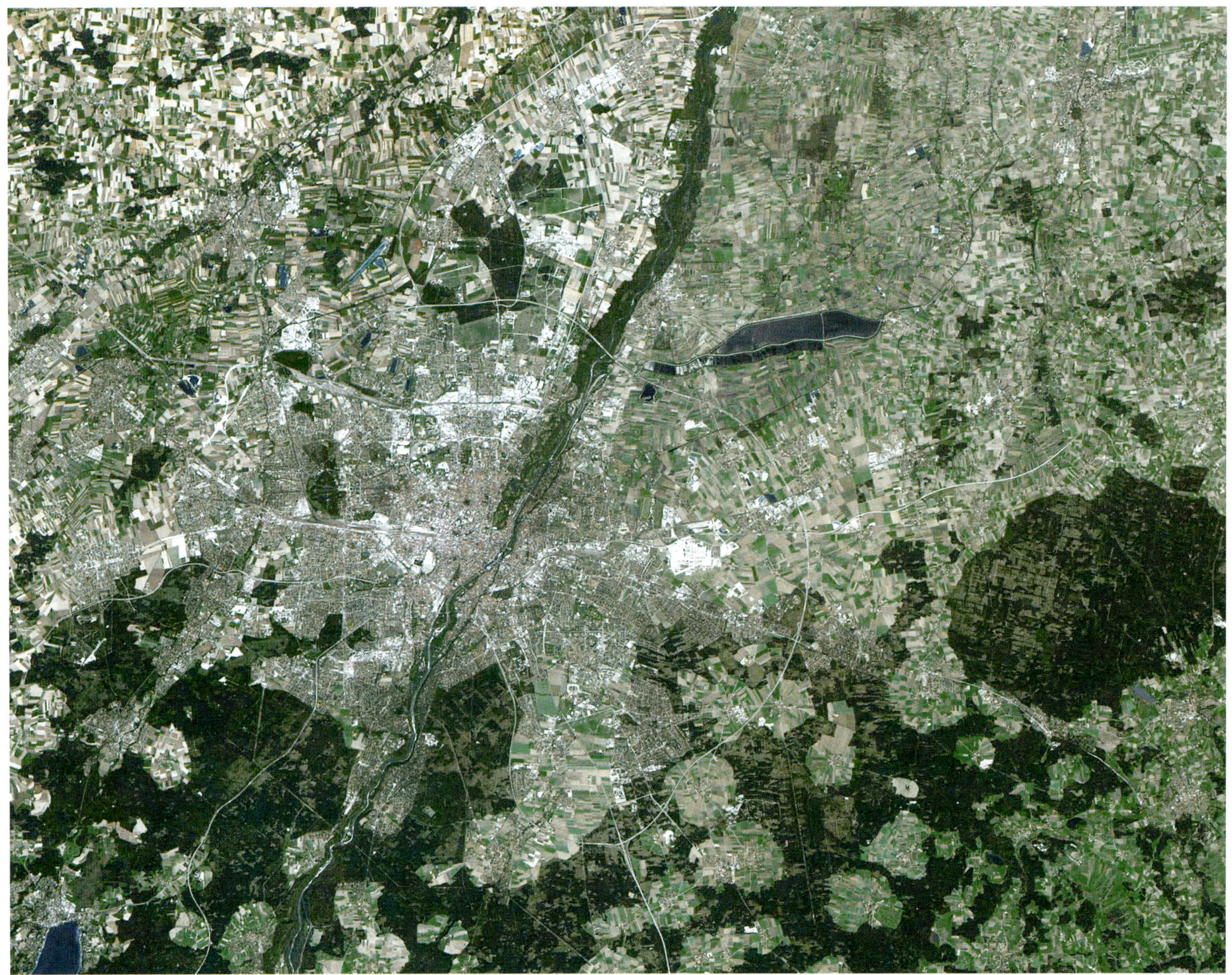

Client Pinakothek der Moderne, Munich
Project Image and communications concepts, catalogues, opening events, bar and bistro, information system for entrance.

Brief The Pinakothek der Moderne is a new, international quality multi-disciplinary museum for the art and design of the 20th and 21st centuries. It brings together four major collections. Its paintings come from the collection of the Staatsgemäldesammlungen, works on paper from the Staatliche Graphische Sammlung, architectural material from the Architekturmuseum TU Munich, and design and applied art from the

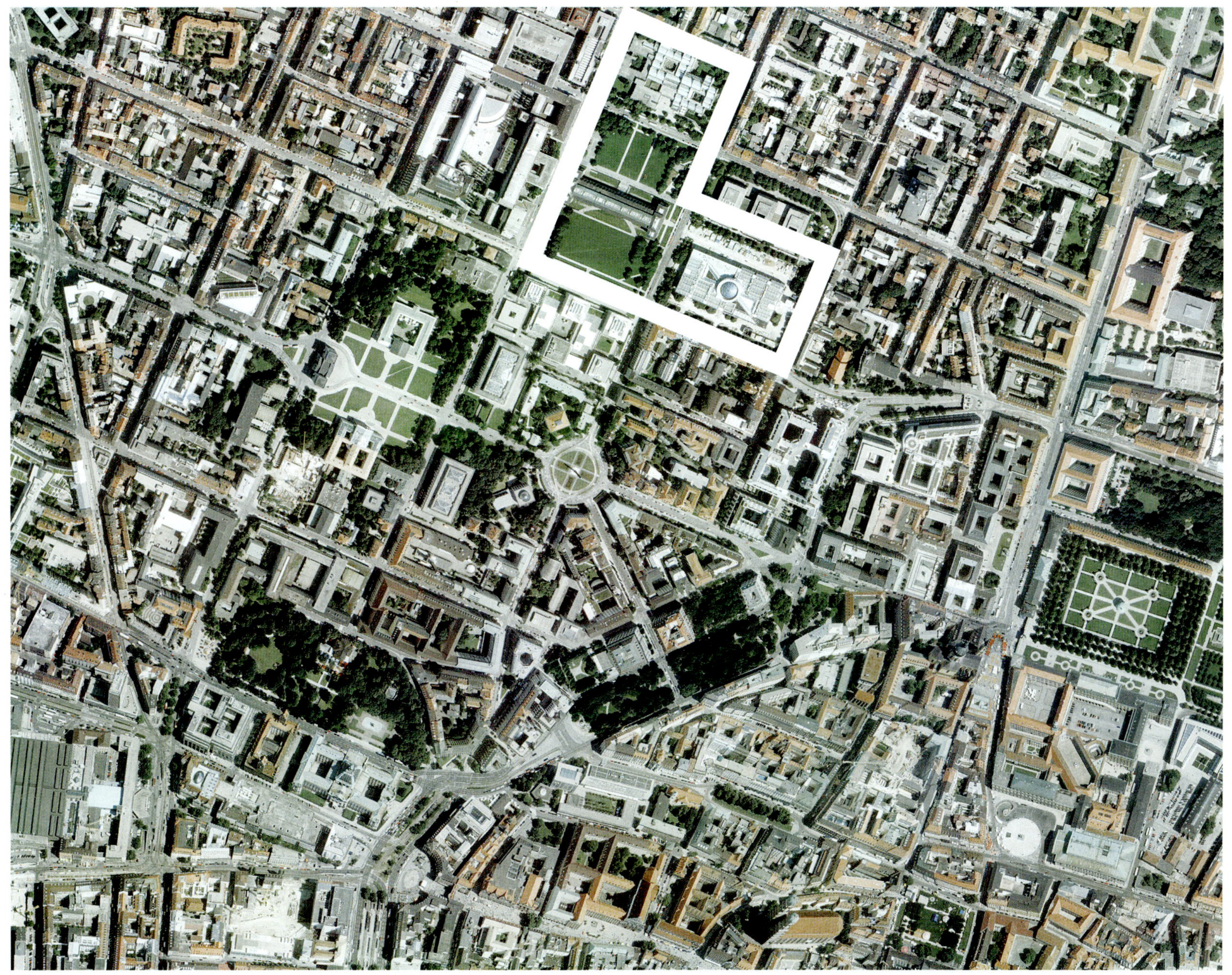

1: 8 700
KUNSTAREAL
MÜNCHEN

Neue Sammlung. For the opening in September 2002 KMS was asked to work on the image of the museum, its communication and information design and on the concepts for the bar and restaurant.

Concept: Munich now has three Pinakotheks (the Alte and Neue Pinakotheks hold the city's excellent collections of Old Master paintings, 14th to 18th century in the Alte, 19th in the Neue.) The new identity concept has therefore had to be applied across all three in a logical and systematic way. For the Alte Pinakothek the symbol is a closed rectangle, and for the Neue an open one, reflecting how the art of the 19th century both drew on the art of the past and opened new perspectives. The logo for the Pinakothek der Moderne deconstructs this notion into the four areas represented in its collections, a motif which also recognises the

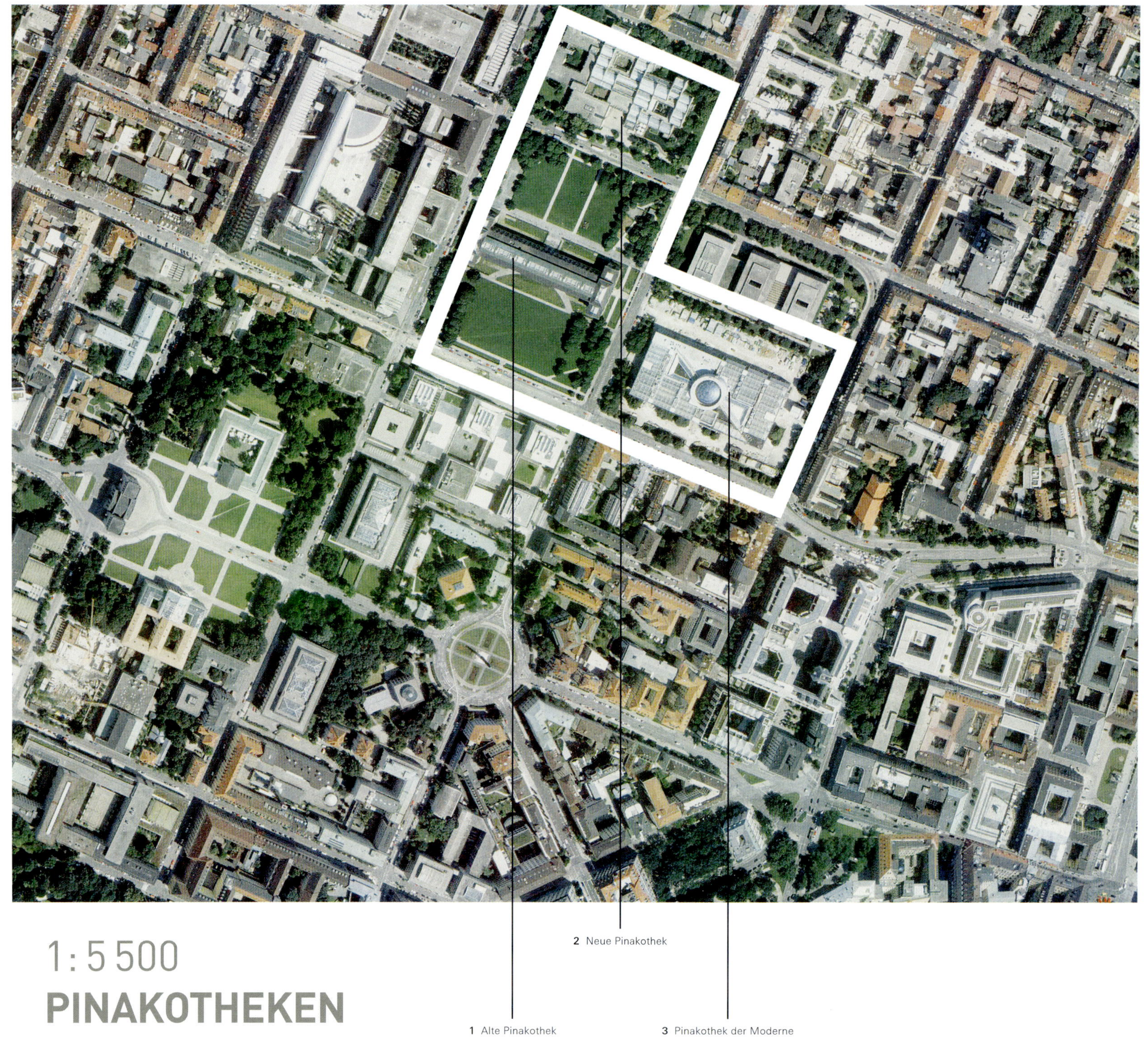

1 : 5 500
PINAKOTHEKEN

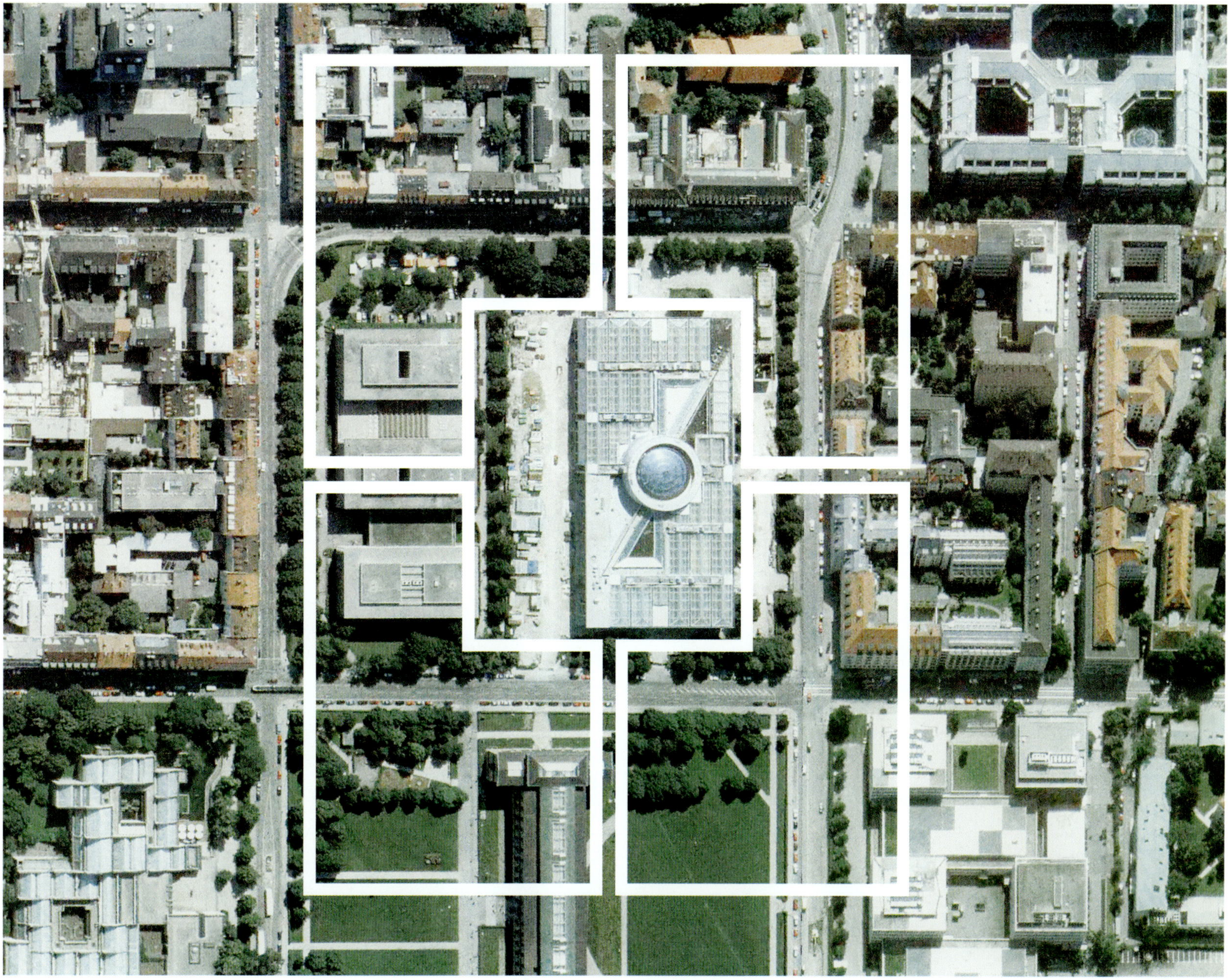

1 : 2 800
PINAKOTHEK DER MODERNE

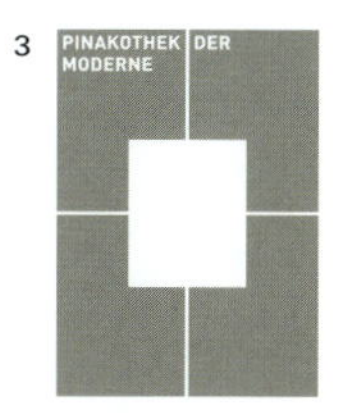

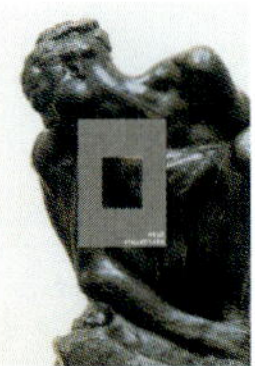

plurality of the contemporary art and design world. The new name 'Kunstareal' for the museum's quarter in Munich draws attention to the exemplary and wide-ranging art collections the city offers to the world. Within the Pinakothek der Moderne's own identity the four constituent elements can be used as sub-logos for the individual collections on catalogues and posters. A grey tone was chosen as the corporate colour, both for its neutrality and to reflect the distinctive colour of the exterior of the new building. The lettering selected for signage and printed materials was similarly classical and sober. For the opening campaign KMS created a series of images using the logo as a window, but figuratively, to appear to show another building or object, and so also echoing the ambiguities between art and reality.

For the catalogues (published by DuMont Verlag) a colour palette was developed both to differentiate different language editions and to specify different types of publication. This classical palette ranges from hot, matt mid-tone colours through to dark pastel shades, analogous to the logo itself and also sufficiently neutral not to contradict the art shown within.

The restaurant is a 12 metre high space on a triangular plan with glazed exterior walls. To integrate it with the museum and its context, a nine-meter cube of translucent fabric is hung from the ceiling on which multimedia and similar works can be projected, visible outside the museum at night, and so providing an additional space for exhibiting such work. The restau-

rant's name 48|8 comes from the geographical latitude of the museum but also extends the four-part concept of the Pinakothek.

Above Rotunda at the Pinakothek der Moderne
Below left Poster series for the three Pinakotheks

Comments The Pinakothek project is a particularly good example of an integrated design scheme. In addition to the aspects mentioned, KMS also advised on naming issues, the design of the museum's contemporary art magazine, and the new identity for the PIN, the friends of the Pinakothek. They also developed the concept for the new website and supervised the competition for the detailed design work. They also developed the overall concept of the Musterraum, a space in which Gate 11, a media studio, presents an international programme of music and video art.

Left Design principle with logo elements
Right Opening campaign for the Pinakothek der Moderne

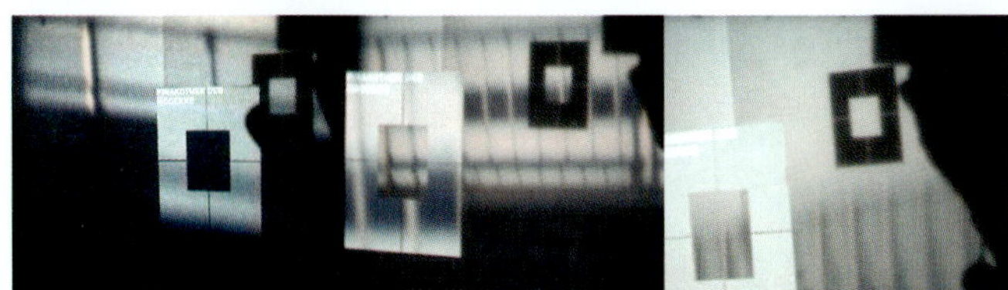

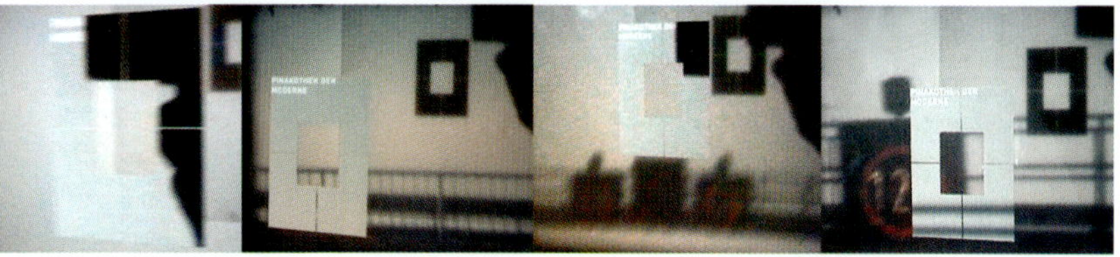

People

A group of Polar explorers, walking wearily across the icecap in the Artic twilight, realised that every time they tried to count their number, there always seemed to be one person more present than was the case.

People Ask many designers about where a design solution originates and they will often say they have no idea, or offer a retrospective survey, back to the scribble on a napkin, and say 'it happened there.' They believe that sincerely, but it's probably not so. The source of a design lies in the resources brought to bear on the challenge of the brief. These can be material—libraries and market researches, materials information and databases—but are in fact very largely human: the experiences, memories and skills of the team and their encounter with previous projects and other clients and other designers: after all a design office is more than a collection of people, but it begins as a collection of people, sharing ideas and concepts.

That said, sometimes designs do not work, or never happen, simply because the resources needed are not there, or the language between client and designer becomes so impenetrable that nothing moves forward at all. Equally, there are times when the client's disbelief is overcome by events.

One of the skills a designer needs is to manage resources (as all the books tell us.) But this has also the specific sense of understanding the strengths and limitations of him or herself, and of colleagues. And also of the client. The brief set by the client is one source for the final design, but what it says about the problem to be solved may be the way to a solution, just as what it does not say may be a guide to the client's view of the situation. Establishing an understanding between designer and client enriches the content and so the context of a project.

O₂
Best in Class

11.09.1999
Presentation of a new
fair stand concept to
VIAG Interkom

02.25.2000
VIAG Interkom stand
wins iF Award, CeBIT
2001

04.26.2001
VIAG Interkom
stand wins iF Award,
CeBIT 2001

11.21.2001
VIAG Interkom stand
wins Adam Award,
CeBIT 2001

11.09. 1999

VIAG Interkom

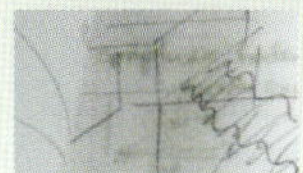

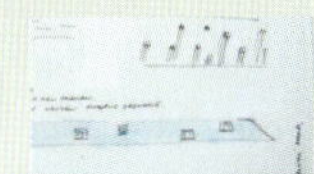

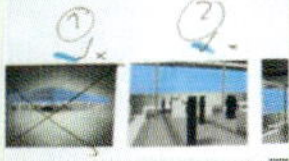

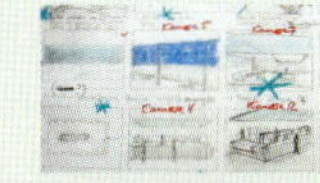
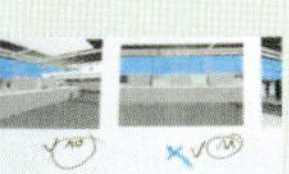

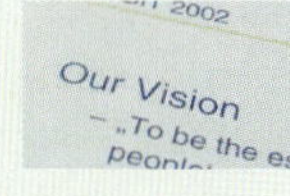

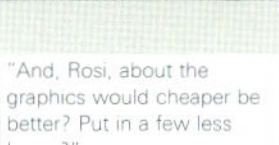
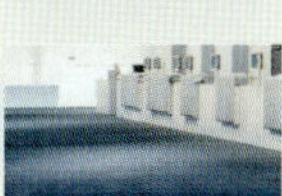

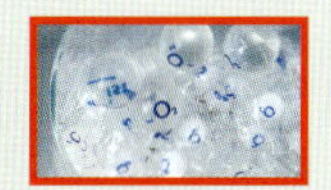

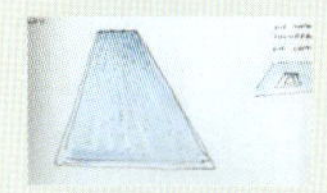

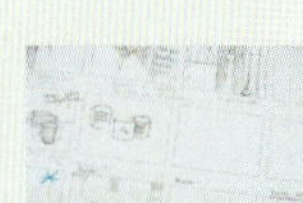
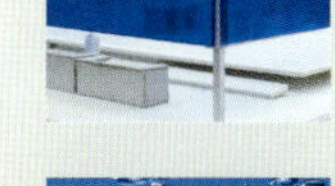

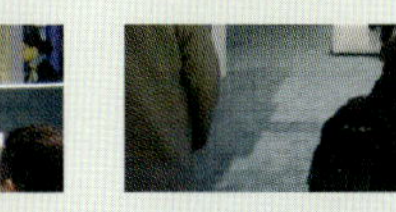

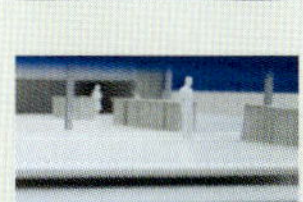

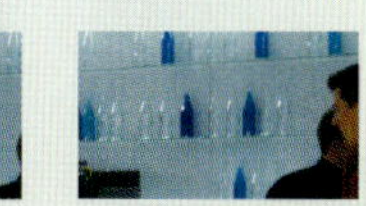

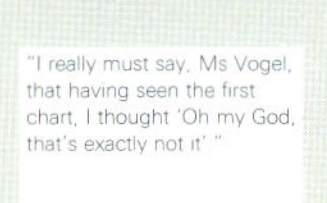

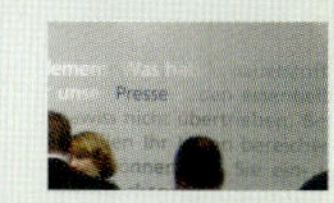

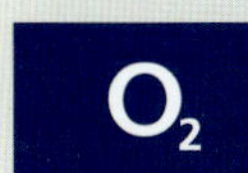

03.14. 2002

O₂ Germany

Client VIAG Interkom/O_2 Germany, Munich
Project Exhibition stand at CeBIT 2002, Hanover

Brief The stand should show the transition from VIAG Interkom to O_2, communicate the new brand to the public, and present the new company as a Europe-wide enterprise dedicated to the mobile telephone market.

Concept The new name links to the chemical sign for oxygen, and in turn to the brand values of clarity, openness, boldness and trust, which were to be presented across all aspects of the stand. KMS had designed prize-winning stands for VIAG in the previous years, with a central concept of a place of calm in the turbulence of the fair. This was to be used again to present the new company to clients. Blue was the corporate colour of the new brand, and so became the key visual colour for the stand, in the form of prominent patterns of bubbles of air in water. The idea was for the overall presentation area to 'hover' some 50 centimetres over the rectangular base. A banner around the inside of the stand, perforated with a grid pattern, and lit by gobos and light presentations, created a virtual horizon over the four inner sides. An extended infobar ran down the centre of the stand, with lounges for more detailed presentations of products and services grouped on each side. Above the bar was a large banner on which images of bubbles were projected. Monitors around the stand also informed visitors about the new brand and its qualities. It was particularly important to make visitors welcome, and for them to feel connected with the new company. This was achieved through details such as carpeting, room layouts and visitor areas.

Comments The new concept was the first to be presented to the client, and was—unusually, in that the client was at first expecting something quite different —executed almost exactly as first proposed, thanks to the confident and established working relationship between KMS and O_2 (formerly VIAG Interkom).

11.14. 2001

Digital preview of
the stand

Direkter Zugang
zu mobilen
Diensten

03.14. 2002
The stand as built

Elegantes
Design
o2
Direkter Zugang
zu mobilen
Diensten
08:30   a.m.
Opening time

14:30 p. m.
Business as usual

10:30 a.m.
Bowl with give-aways

04.30.2002
Event in the Radsport-
halle to show the look
of the new stand to O_2
colleagues from Munich
and Nuremberg.

05.01.2002
The O_2 brand officially
launched in Germany

06.04.2002
The adapted design first
shown at Mobil World
fair, Berlin

06.07.2002
KMS appointed as
official corporate design
agency for O_2 Germany

06.18.2002
Re-organisation of
the company's
headquarters in Munich
completed.

Further events for O_2
colleagues in Berlin,
Bremen and Cologne

The CeBIT design is adopted
for smaller scale fairs

07.09.2002
Partnership between
O_2 Germany and
Pinakothek der Moderne

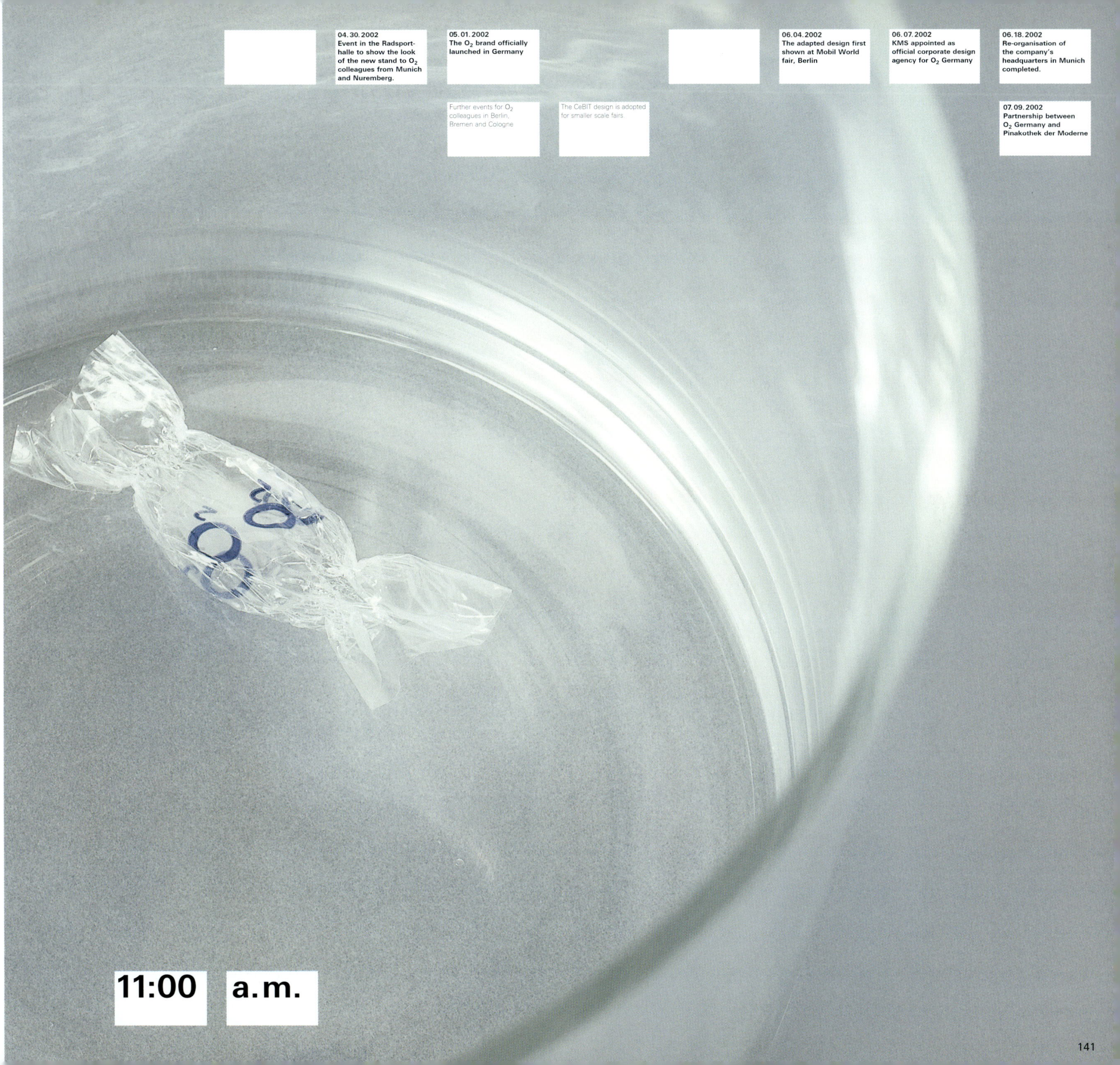

11:00   a.m.

Source

"Designers should read about everything except design."
Philippe Starck

Source Ask a design company what their list of projects is, and there is always one that they leave out. As often as not, it is one of the most important ones, it is certainly of long duration, and no client confidentiality is involved. It is, quite simply, the project of the design company itself, its nature, development, potential and identity.
So this book has not been about KMS, in fact. It has had to be about KMS as a project. To describe KMS in detail might be anecdotally entertaining but also extremely lengthy and finally meaningless (as Roland Barthes so elegantly discovered in writing about Japan.) So I have set out to describe in part what I feel a good design company should be, and in part what I think KMS is and what it does. Where the two correlate I leave to the reader to judge from the work, and the whole. What I have to say has been shaped by talking to the people at KMS, watching them at work and looking at their work, and by talking to many other designers and looking at and reading about design and designers. This is something I find fascinating, and beyond that pleasure, I believe it to be relevant and important in a very wide sense.

Because every design is also part of the project of design.

KMS Team   nzinger Str
Sarah-Joan Fuld 089.490
evatec
DANKE

Thursday morning at KMS—the sacral moment. The company breakfast, a meeting without an agenda, a structure with no organisation—apart from a washing-up rota. Cafewissenschaft or rumour mill? There are a few announcements—housekeeping issues, special mentions, awards and staff events. Groups form and reform around the benches and tables, over tea and coffee, croissants and pretzels. A bonding exercise or a gossip conference?

Events like this happen in a lot of design companies. Sometimes formally, such as award schemes that review and reward work on a monthly basis, sometimes informally, through a softball team or a cookery club. Does it work at KMS? It seems so. The proof is that every Thursday the knockout league and team board for the in-house table football tournament is scrupulously updated. Given that the scoring system makes baseball statistics seem childishly simple, no wonder it takes everybody a couple of hours.

But life at KMS is not just about having fun. There is a continuing debate going on within KMS about why and how they work, what their guiding concepts are, a debate that is part of a process of evaluating their results. This is not done formally: KMS doesn't even have a strapline to hang its beliefs on. But spend time in their office, and listen to the work, and the process is there. Take the way the offices are laid out, on the ground floor of an old post office building in the centre of Munich, emphasises the absence of hierarchy that encourages discourse, for example. The main raised area is the client meeting room by the main doors. This is a glass box, unlike the shut-off spaces some agencies choose. It is as if to say that what happens with the clients at KMS happens in everybody's view. As part of the briefing for this book, along with lists of projects and prizes, copies of presentations and files of images, I was given a small pile of folders in which individual members of staff had made notes for me of

what they liked and disliked about working there: I was given strict instructions not to show these to the partners. The folders contained, inter alia, a recipe for paella, a map showing the cycle route from S's apartment to the office, two love poems, several out of focus shots of a party (or perhaps several equally unsteady parties), a postcard of the Golden Gate Bridge, a note thanking everyone for an engagement present, four beer mats from Ibiza in a distressed state, the email address of someone's dog, and two dried flowers.

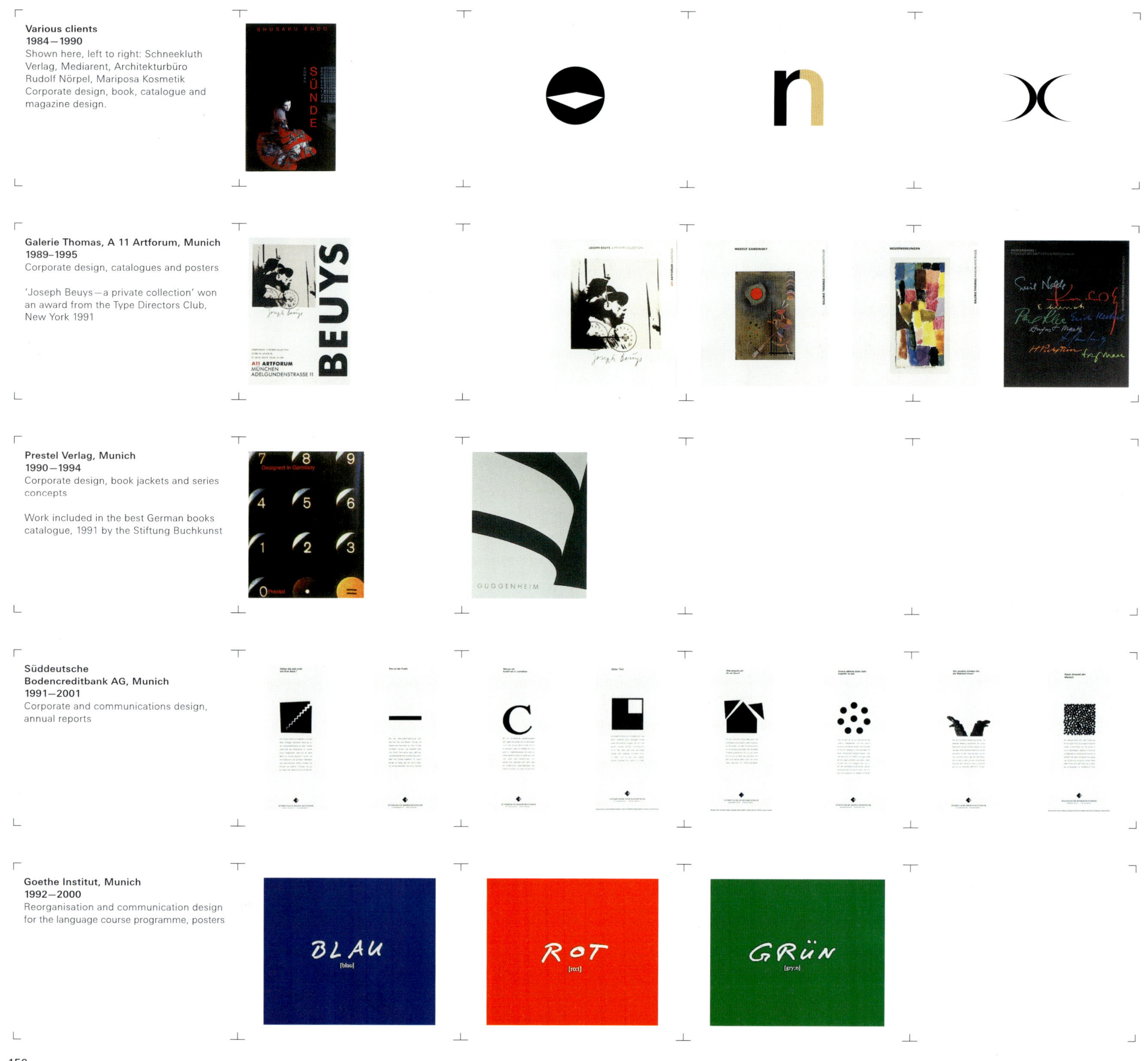

Various clients
1984—1990
Shown here, left to right: Schneekluth
Verlag, Mediarent, Architekturbüro
Rudolf Nörpel, Mariposa Kosmetik
Corporate design, book, catalogue and
magazine design.

Galerie Thomas, A 11 Artforum, Munich
1989—1995
Corporate design, catalogues and posters

'Joseph Beuys—a private collection' won
an award from the Type Directors Club,
New York 1991

Prestel Verlag, Munich
1990—1994
Corporate design, book jackets and series
concepts

Work included in the best German books
catalogue, 1991 by the Stiftung Buchkunst

**Süddeutsche
Bodencreditbank AG, Munich**
1991—2001
Corporate and communications design,
annual reports

Goethe Institut, Munich
1992—2000
Reorganisation and communication design
for the language course programme, posters

Museum Villa Stuck, Munich
1993 to date
Corporate design, posters

Work included in 'Graphis Poster Annual'
for 1995 and 2001

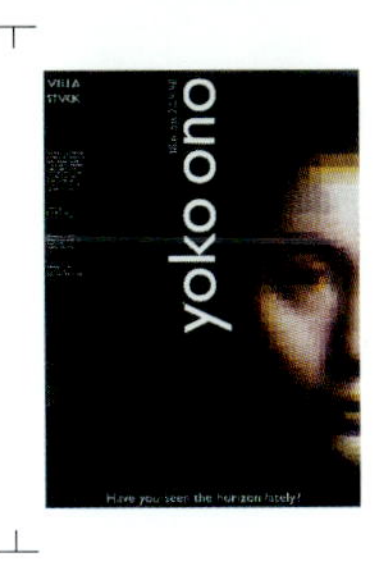

Philip Morris Kunstförderung, Munich
1993 – 1996
Corporate and communication design,
posters and catalogues

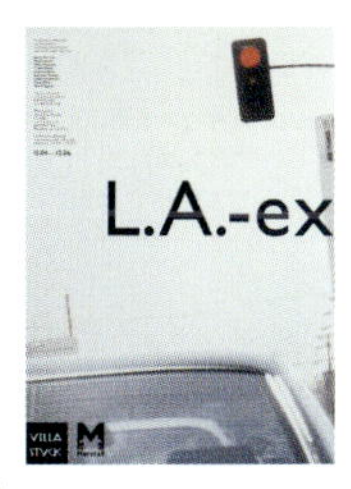

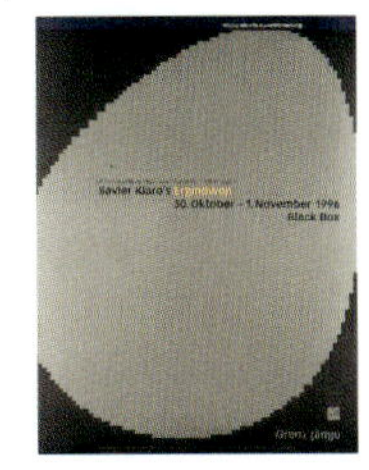

ProSieben Media AG, Munich
1996 – 2000
Corporate design, brand and subbranding,
communication design, annual reports

Rated 'Manager Magazin': Best quoted
newcomer [1996 report], Rated first in
the M-Dax category [1997 report]; Rated
'Capital' third in the M-Dax category
[1998 report], Rated third in the M-Dax
category [1999 report]

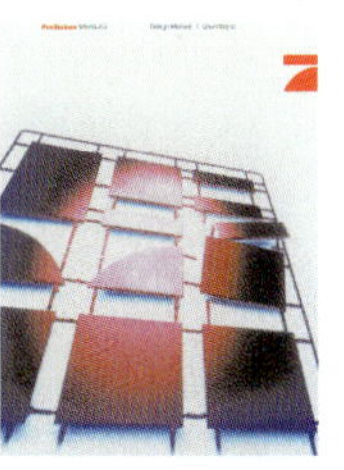

Architekturbüro
Schmidhuber+Partner, Munich
1996 – 1999
Corporate design, presentation systems

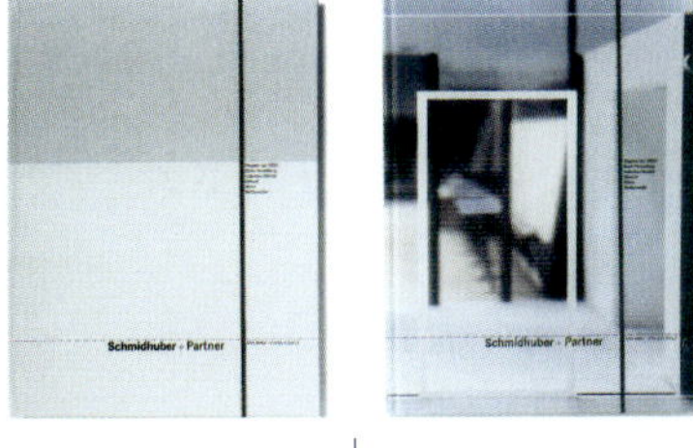

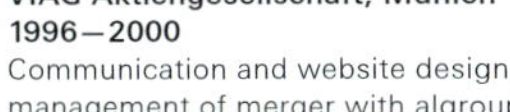

VIAG Aktiengesellschaft, Munich
1996 – 2000
Communication and website design, design
management of merger with algroup

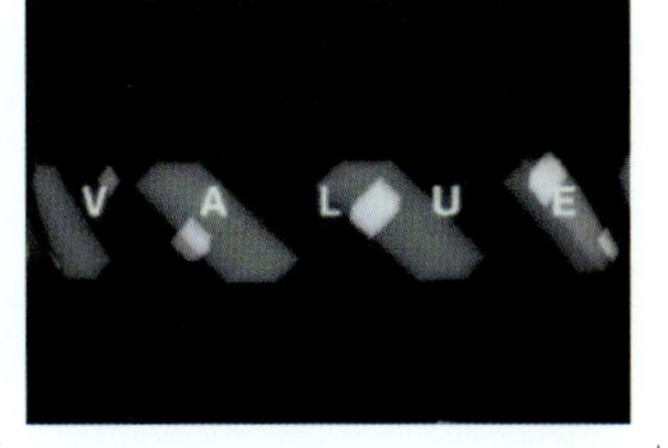

AUDI AG, Ingolstadt
1997—2002
Conception and planning for the A-series
motor shows (Frankfurt, Paris, Detroit,
Geneva, Tokyo)

Stand design for IAA 1997, Frankfurt

iF Industrie Forum Design Hanover:
Silver Award for Exhibition Design 1997

Stand design for Mondial de l'Automobile
1998, Paris

Deutscher Preis für Kommunikationsdesign
2000: design quality award

Stand design for IAA 1999, Frankfurt

iF Industrie Forum Design Hanover: silver
award for Exhibition Design 1999
Deutscher Preis für Kommunikationsdesign
2000: design quality award for the
A2 installation; Berliner Type 2000: silver
medal for visitor's pack.

Film component in stand design IAA 1999,
Frankfurt

ADC Deutschland 2000: award;
Ars Electronica 2000: award;
Deutscher Preis für Kommunikationsdesign
2000: award for high design quality

Stand design IAA 2001, Frankfurt and
NAIAS 2002, Detroit

DIO Award 2002 for Most Significant
Exhibit Design [Detroit]

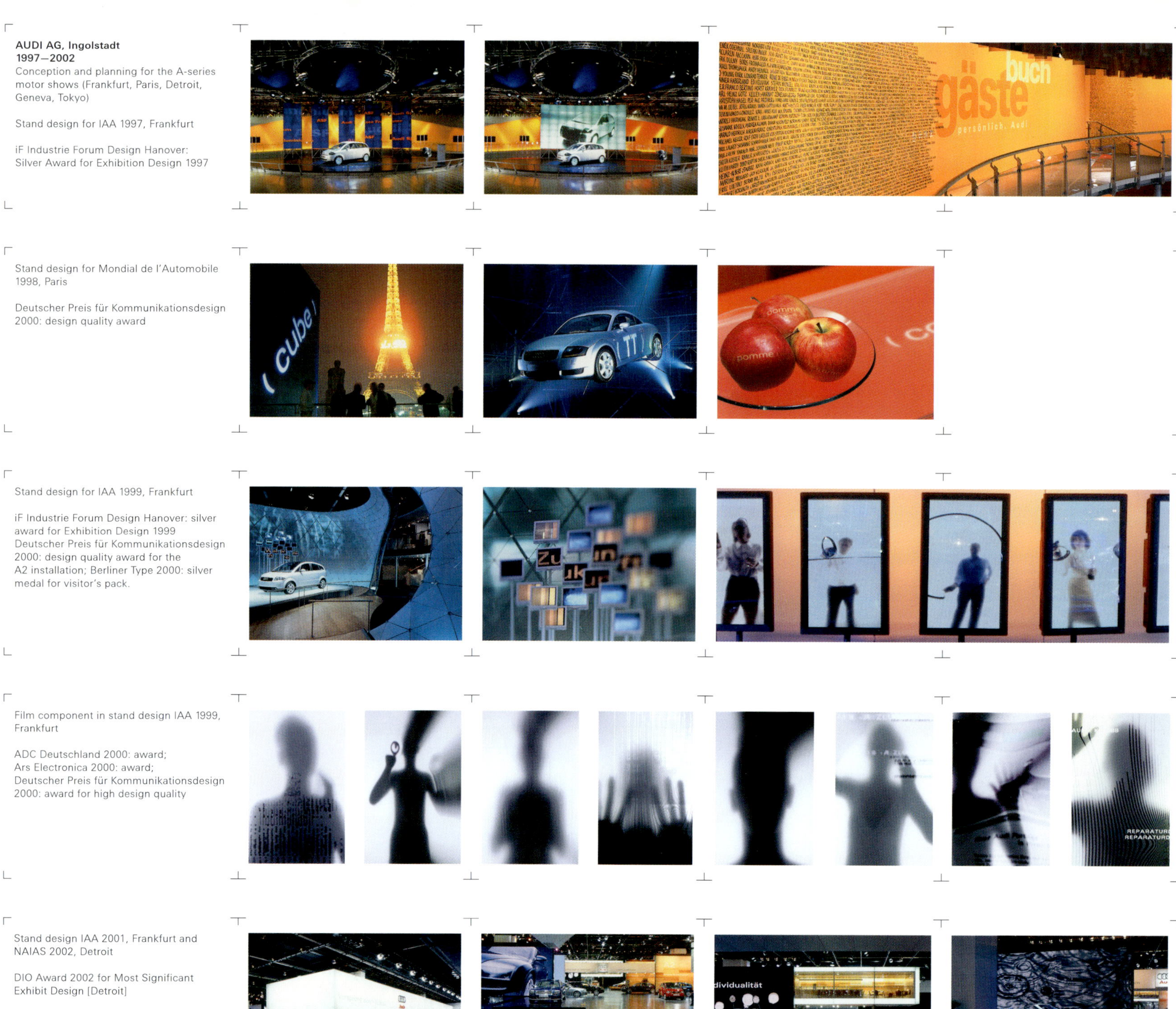

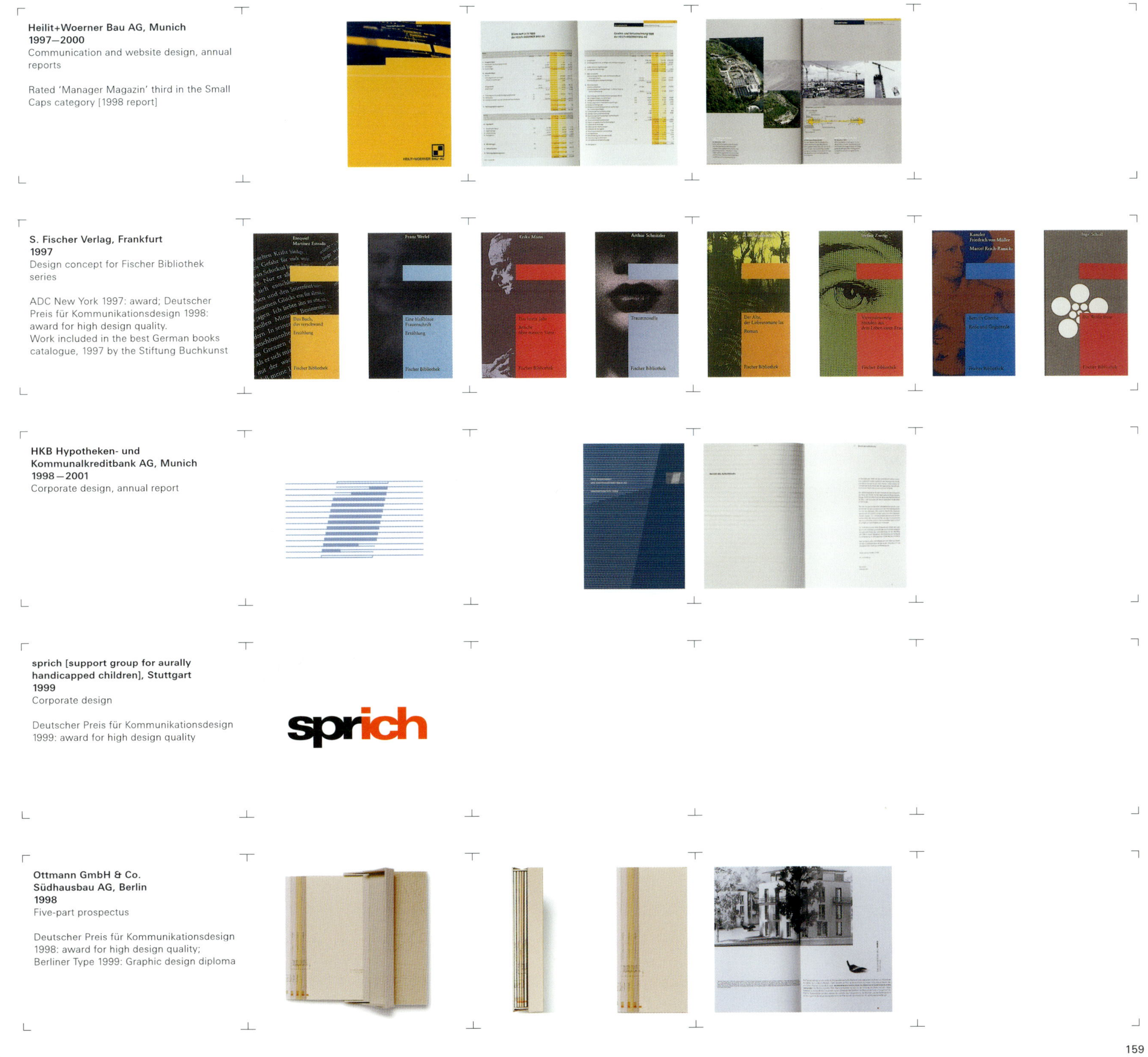

Heilit+Woerner Bau AG, Munich
1997—2000
Communication and website design, annual
reports

Rated 'Manager Magazin' third in the Small
Caps category [1998 report]

S. Fischer Verlag, Frankfurt
1997
Design concept for Fischer Bibliothek
series

ADC New York 1997: award; Deutscher
Preis für Kommunikationsdesign 1998:
award for high design quality.
Work included in the best German books
catalogue, 1997 by the Stiftung Buchkunst

HKB Hypotheken- und
Kommunalkreditbank AG, Munich
1998 —2001
Corporate design, annual report

sprich [support group for aurally
handicapped children], Stuttgart
1999
Corporate design

Deutscher Preis für Kommunikationsdesign
1999: award for high design quality

Ottmann GmbH & Co.
Südhausbau AG, Berlin
1998
Five-part prospectus

Deutscher Preis für Kommunikationsdesign
1998: award for high design quality;
Berliner Type 1999: Graphic design diploma

**museum mobile AUDI AG, Ingolstadt
1998—2000**
Project concept, corporate and
communication design, naming

ADC New York 2001: silver award;
red dot award 2001: Grand Prix;
iF design award 2002: award; Classic
Cars magazine competition:
Museum of the Year 2001; The New York
Festivals 2001: Finalist Certificate;
Corporate Design Preis 2001: award

for website and catalogue

ADC Deutschland 2001: bronze award;
Berliner Type 2001: silver award [for the
Museum catalogue];
iF design award 2002: silver award
[for the website]

**Automobili Lamborghini S.p. A., Bologna
1998 to date**
Corporate design, showrooms and stand
design

ADAM Award 2001: third prize for foreign
exhibition stands [Motor Show 1999,
Bologna]; contractworld award 2001: Gold
in the Shops/Showrooms category [for the
stand at IAA 2001, Frankfurt]

Product launch of the Murciélago at Etna,
name development and positioning

EIBTM-Award 2002: Best Event in Europe

**Museum Charlotte Zander,
Sammlung für naive Kunst, Bönnigheim
1997**
Corporate design

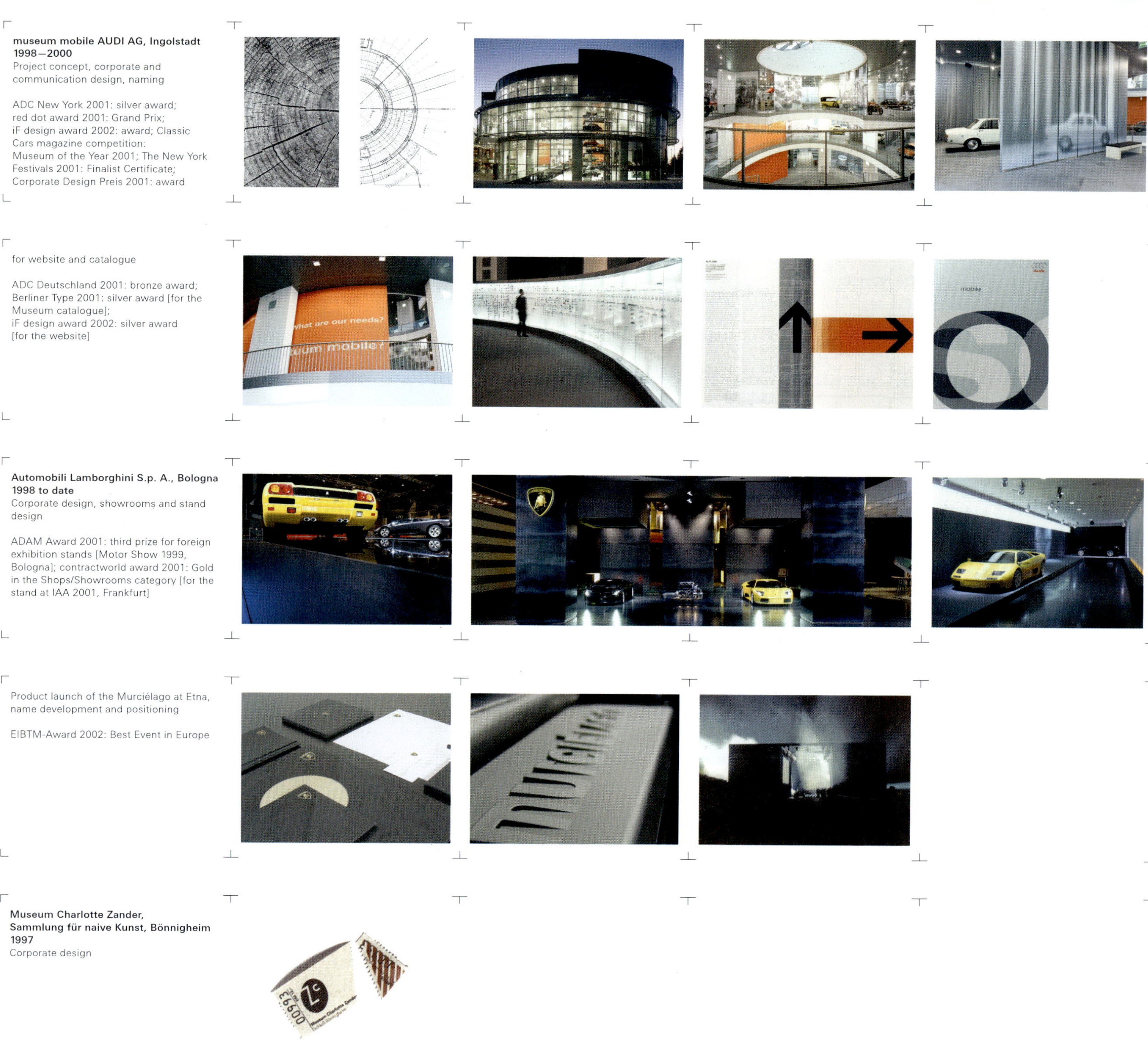

Evotec BioSystems AG, Hamburg
1999
Annual report

Rated 'Capital' first in the Nemax
category; The New York Festivals 2000:
Finalist Certificate

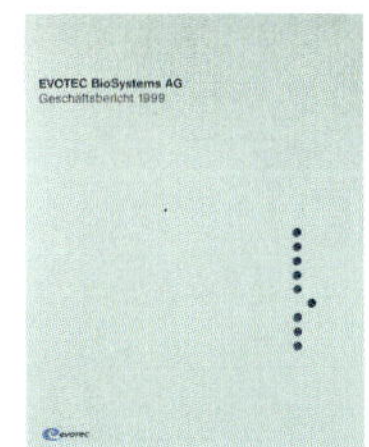 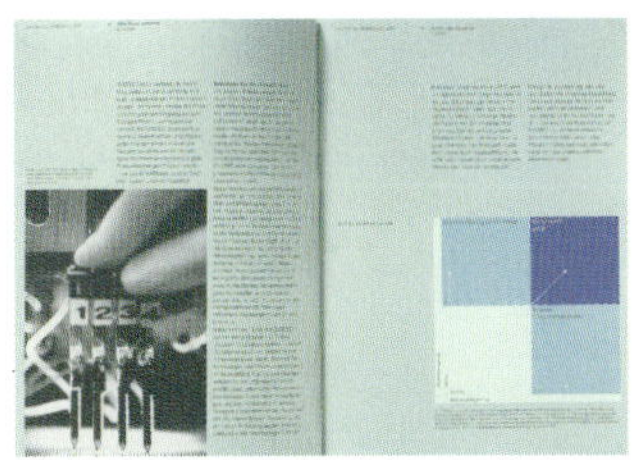 

compær AG, Munich
1999—2000
Corporate and communication design,
naming, website design

Included in 'Graphis Letterheads 5', 2001

  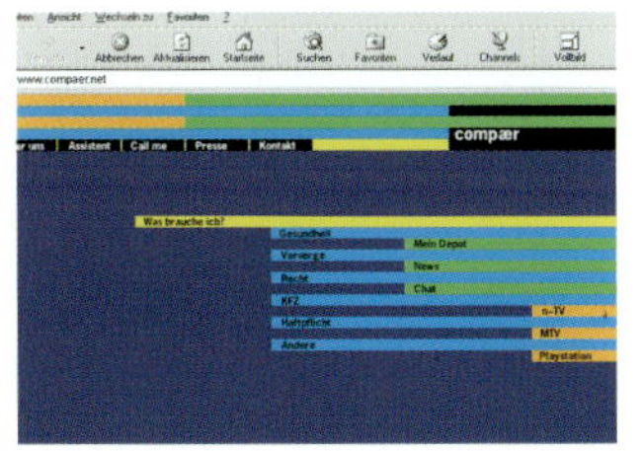 

VIAG Interkom, Munich
1999 to date
Conception and execution of stand designs

Stand design CeBIT 2000, Hanover

iF Industrie Forum Design Hanover:
Gold Award for Exhibition Design, 2000

Stand design CeBIT 2001, Hanover

iF Industrie Forum Design Hanover:
Gold Award for Exhibition Design, 2001;
ADAM Award 2001: second prize in
the under 1,500 square metre stand
group; iF design award 2001: award

Saturn, Ingolstadt
1999
New logo design

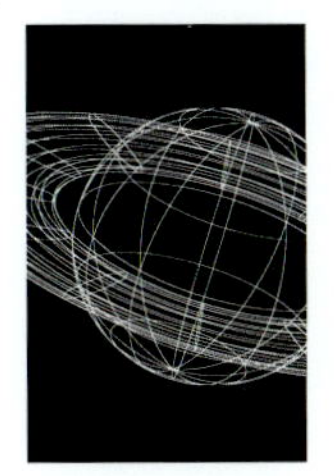   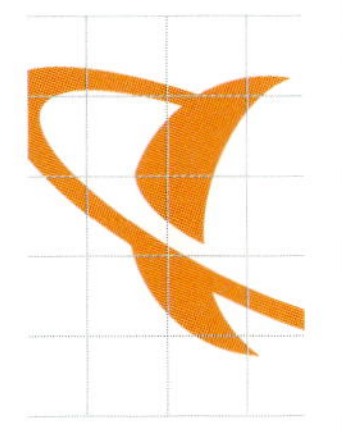 

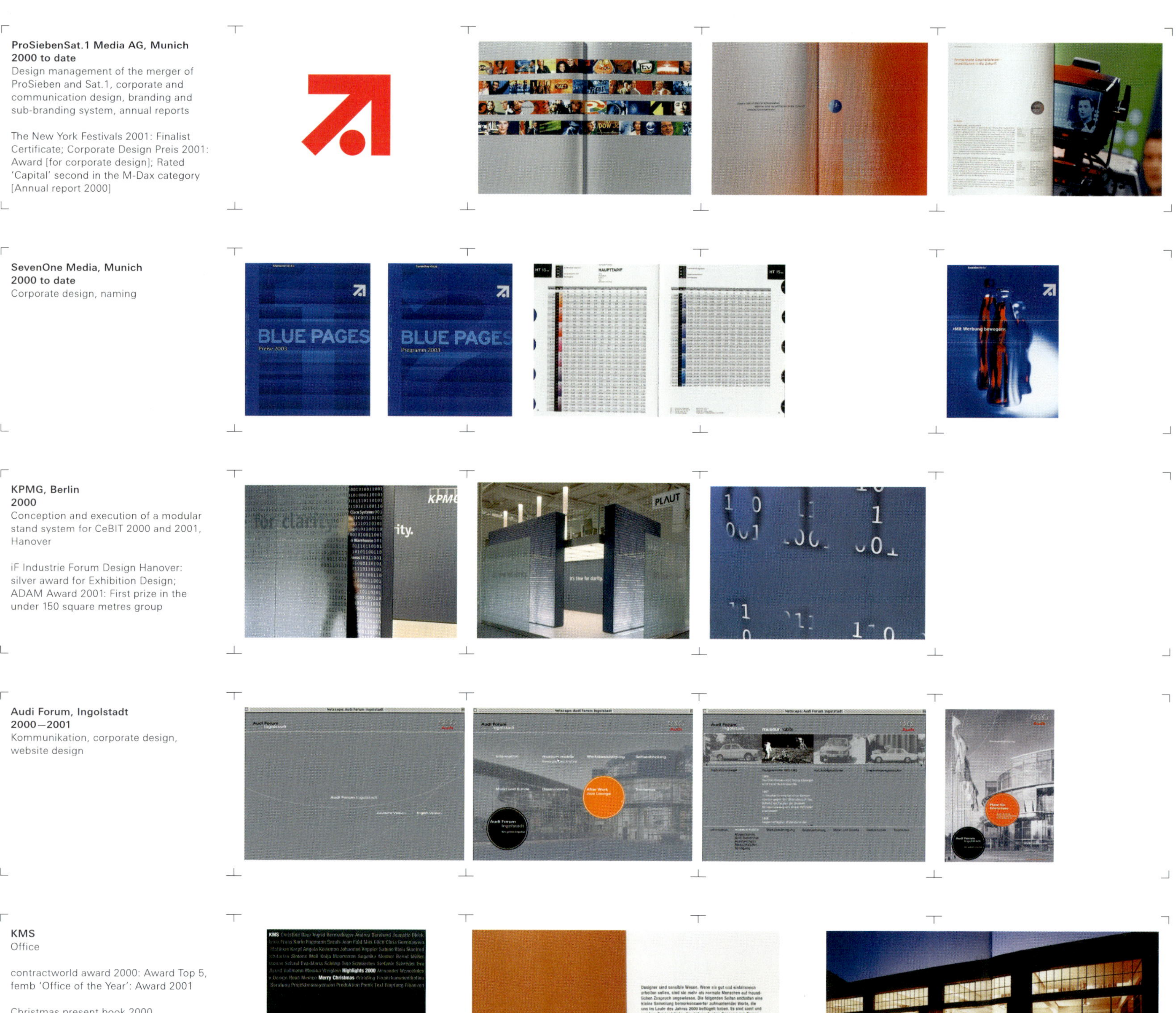

ProSiebenSat.1 Media AG, Munich
2000 to date
Design management of the merger of ProSieben and Sat.1, corporate and communication design, branding and sub-branding system, annual reports

The New York Festivals 2001: Finalist Certificate; Corporate Design Preis 2001: Award [for corporate design]; Rated 'Capital' second in the M-Dax category [Annual report 2000]

SevenOne Media, Munich
2000 to date
Corporate design, naming

KPMG, Berlin
2000
Conception and execution of a modular stand system for CeBIT 2000 and 2001, Hanover

iF Industrie Forum Design Hanover: silver award for Exhibition Design; ADAM Award 2001: First prize in the under 150 square metres group

Audi Forum, Ingolstadt
2000—2001
Kommunikation, corporate design, website design

KMS
Office

contractworld award 2000: Award Top 5, femb 'Office of the Year': Award 2001

Christmas present book 2000

ADC Deutschland 2001: bronze award

Evotec OAI AG, Hamburg, Oxford
2000 to date
Design management for merger between
Evotec and Oxford Asymmetry
International, Corporate and
communications design, annual reports

Corporate Design Preis 2001: Award for the
identity; 'Capital' and 'Manager Magazin'
ranked third in the Nemax category for the
2000 annual report; The New York Festivals
2001: Finalist Certificate [also for the
2000 report]

Annual report 2001

LACP Award 2002: Silver Award

Kirch Gruppe, Munich
2000 to date
Corporate design, branding system, Annual
reports for KirchMedia and KirchPayTV

ADC Deutschland 2001: Award; The New
York Festivals 2001: Silver World Medal;
Berliner Type 2001: Bronze Award [for the
1999 annual report]

Annual report 2000

red dot award 2002: design quality award;
iF design award 2001: Award [for the
2000 annual report]

Ingenhoven Overdiek und Partner
Together with KMS
2001
'1/1. Architecture and Design:
New Synergies.'
Book with an essay by Robert Wilson.
Basel: Birkhäuser 2001

iF design award 2002: award

KMS was founded in 1984, initially as a graphic design studio, and in the following years extended its range to include both financial documentation, such as annual reports, and exhibition and trade fair stand design. By the middle of the 1990s, with their competence established, KMS specialised in all aspects of corporate identity work, including strategic planning, branding and naming, corporate culture and language, three-dimensional design and website design, in an integrated range of services. Today KMS, under the leadership of Michael Keller, Knut Maierhofer (founder) and Christoph Rohrer, is among the top ten design offices in Germany.

KMS Team GmbH | Deroystraße 3–5 | D-80335 Munich | www.kms-team.de
Tel. 00 49.89.490 411-0 | Fax 00 49.89.490 411-49 | ISDN 00 49.89.490 411-17 | info@kms-team.de

Michael Keller, Knut Maierhofer, Christoph Rohrer | Christina Baur, Sabine Berens, Ingrid Bermadinger, Jeanette Bleck, Thorsten Buch, Hannes Dölker, Tom Ferraro, Marion Fink, Sabine Huber, Ralph Ilsanker, Julia Just, Matthias Karpf, Angela Keesman, Constanze Knoesel, Peta Kobrow, Stefanie Kochbeck, Judith Leister, Bruno Marek, Patrick Märki, Wahan Mechitarian, Kolja Moormann, Angelika Mosner, Bernd Müller, Norman Müller, Sonja Ney, Marco Peters, Christian Ring, Ludwig Robert, Eva Rohrer, Cecil Rustemeyer, Dr. Axel Sanjosé, Armin Schlamp, Eva-Maria Schleip, Stefanie Schröder, Stefan Schwarz, Sven Sonnendorfer, Sabine Thernes, Isabelle Valina, Birgit Vogel, Carolin Welß, Bernhard Zölch | Uli Aldinger, Jörg Bruppacher, Katja Egloff, Chris Goennawein, Timo Meyer, Melanie Sauer, Julia Schibler

KMS would like to extend its warmest thanks to the following:
Michael Bock, Wilfried Munk, Tina Hubbert, Stefan Glaser, Robert Ehmann, Ives Carpentier, Gabriele Fanta, Jens Thiemer, Waltraud Hinterkopf, Martin Fuchs (DaimlerChrysler AG) | Jörn Aldag, Dr. Karsten Henco, Anne Hennecke (Evotec OAI AG) | Dorothee Seeliger (Hallwag Verlag) | Hartmut Schultz (KirchMedia GmbH & Co. KGaA) | Giuseppe Greco, Bernd Hoffmann, Manfred Fitzgerald, Luc Donckerwolke (Automobili Lamborghini) | Dr. Rainer Hecker, Thomas Bender, Peter Weil (Loewe) | Rudolf J. Gröger, Stefan Zuber, Brigitte Graf, Oliver Biem, Ulrike Pelz, Mike Schwanke, Christina Krenzler [O$_2$ (Germany) GmbH & Co. OHG] | Prof. Dr. Reinhold Baumstark, Prof. Dr. Florian Hufnagl, Prof. Dr. Winfried Nerdinger, Prof. Dr. Carla Schulz-Hoffmann, Dr. Michael Semff (Pinakothek der Moderne) | Urs Rohner, Dr. Torsten Rossmann (ProSiebenSat.1 Media AG) | Jo-Anne Birnie Danzker, Michael Buhrs (Museum Villa Stuck)

Author's thanks
In writing this book I did not feel I was on the outside, writing about KMS, more that I was part of a team creating a KMS project. It has been an enthralling and rewarding experience, for which I thank deeply everyone at KMS. But there must also be a special word of thanks for Axel Sanjosé, who undertook to translate my texts for the German edition: diolch a chwi, Axel, or rather, moltes gràcies.
Conway Lloyd Morgan, Chez le Pauvre, July, 2002.

Imprint

Die Deutsche Bibliothek – CIP-Einheitsaufnahme
KMS : twelve chapters about a design office / Conway Lloyd Morgan. – Ludwigsburg : av-Ed., 2002 (av-Edition rockets)
Dt. Ausg. u. d. T. : KMS

ISBN 3-929638-68-1

Design: KMS | Sabine Berens, Tom Ferraro, Bruno Marek, Stefanie Schröder, Carolin Welß, Uli Aldinger

Editorial: KMS | Axel Sanjosé

Editorial assistance: KMS | Judith Leister

Copyediting: Vineeta Manglani

Project management: KMS | Ingrid Bermadinger, Eva-Maria Schleip

DTP: KMS | Angela Keesman

Production: KMS | Stefan Schwarz
avcommunication AG | Corinna Rieber, Manuela Bloss, Gunther Heeb

Printed by Leibfarth & Schwarz GmbH & Co. KG, Dettingen/Erms

Photos
Uli Aldinger [146–151], Victor S. Brigola [152, 153], Jens Bruchhaus [12, 13, 34, 52, 53, 86–91, 132, 133, 140, 141], Jörg Bruppacher [135, 146–151], Hans-Georg Esch [96–99], Chris Goennawein [103, 108, 109, 146–151], Andreas Keller [96–99], Sabine Klein [48, 49, 96–99], Knut Koops [124, 125, 127], Stefan Müller-Naumann [80, 81, 134, 135, 137, 138], Vera Novottny [96–99], Radical Images [76, 77], Albert van Rosendaal [96–99], TravelTainment [120–123], Marek Vogel [96–99], Birgit Vogel [135, 139]

Photos Appendix
Jens Bruchhaus, Hans-Georg Esch, Andreas Keller, Eva Nieberle, Stefan Müller-Naumann, Vera Novottny, Albert van Rosendaal, Jens Weber

avedition GmbH
Verlag für Architektur und Design
Königsallee 57
71638 Ludwigsburg
www.avedition.de
kontakt@avedition.de

ISBN 3-929638-68-1
Printed in Germany